THE LUFTWAFFE IN AFRICA, 1941–1943

CASEMATE | ILLUSTRATED

CASEMATE | ILLUSTRATED

THE LUFTWAFFE IN AFRICA, 1941–1943

JEAN-LOUIS ROBA

CASEMATE | ILLUSTRATED

Author's thanks: Special thanks for assistance in the provision of photos: Zeno Bäumel (+), Hubert Greim, Karl-Otto Holzapfel, Wolf-Dieter Huy (+), Eduard Neumann (+), Reinhold Omert (+), Neil Page, Peter Taghon, Family von Kageneck, Matti Salonen, Rudolf Sinner (+), Family Wehmeyer, Werner Zirus (+).

CIS0015

Print Edition: ISBN 978-1-61200-7458
Digital Edition: ISBN 978-1-61200-7465

All images from author's collection

Text by Jean-Louis Roba
Translation by Neil Page
Profiles by Vincent Dhorne
Design by Battlefield Design
Printed and bound by Megaprint, Turkey

CASEMATE PUBLISHERS (US)
Telephone (610) 853-9131
Fax (610) 853-9146
Email: casemate@casematepublishers.com
www.casematepublishers.com

CASEMATE PUBLISHERS (UK)
Telephone (01865) 241249
Fax (01865) 794449
Email: casemate-uk@casematepublishers.co.uk
www.casematepublishers.co.uk

Title page: The Luftwaffe quickly established a permanent presence on the Derna plateau, an ideal location for an airfield. Here a Bf 110 of III./ZG 26 prepares to escort a fleet of Ju 52s.
Contents page: This Bf 109 E still wears much of its European camouflage.
Map: Airfields used by the Luftwaffe in Libya and Egypt.

Note: vehicle illustrations and profiles are not to scale.

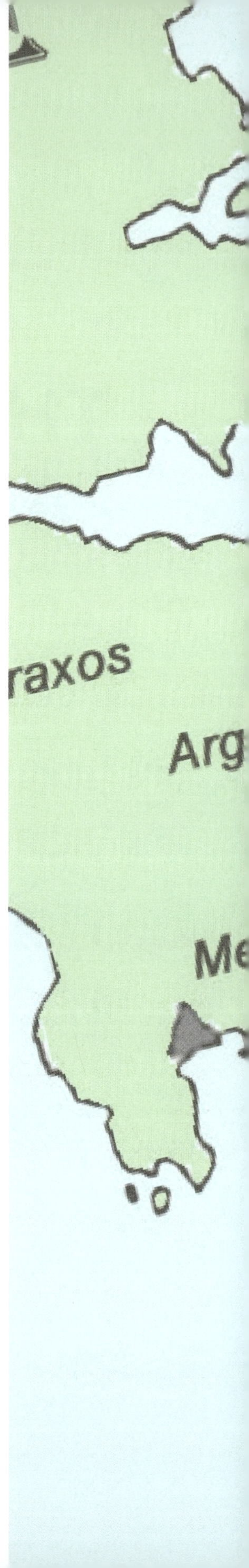

Contents

Timeline of Events

Tobruk harbor seen from a Ju 87.

From the first Luftwaffe action in North Africa—a failed and costly raid on the Suez Canal—on January 17, 1941 through some 30 months of see-saw combat until the Axis forces were finally expelled from Africa in mid-May 1943, the Luftwaffe was at the forefront of hostilities. Continuously haemorrhaging irreplaceable aircraft, and worse, irreplaceable aircrew, many of whom were celebrated veterans and aces, the German air force nevertheless managed to punch considerably above its weight, often against overwhelming odds, such as the advent of the USAAF into the war.

1940

September 13, 1940: Graziano launches Italian offensive against Egypt

1941

January 17, 1941: First Luftwaffe raid in North Africa, on Suez Canal, ends in failure, with 10 aircraft lost

February 6, 1941: Benghazi falls to the British counteroffensive. Rommel forms the Afrika Korps (DAK)

February 12, 1941: Rommel arrives in Tripoli. LG 1 Ju 88s fly first sortie from Sicily

February 19, 1941: Bf 110s claim first Luftwaffe kills on African soil (2 Hurricanes)

April 2, 1941: DAK recaptures Benghazi in Rommel's fresh offensive. "Fortress Tobruk" resists, siege begins

May 10, 1941: Operation *Merkur*, German airborne invasion of Crete

May 16, 1941: Wavell launches Operation *Brevity*, a month later *Battleaxe*; both stall

September 22, 1941: II./JG 27 arrives in theater, as significant fighter reinforcement

October 31, 1941: Kesselring appointed head of Luftflottekommando 2

November 18, 1941: Launch of major British offensive, Operation *Crusader*

1942

January 8, 1942: With Rommel withdrawn to El Agheila; *Crusader* ends with British lines overstretched

4.(H)/12, equipped with Bf 110s and Bf 109s, arrived in the desert in April 1942 to replace 2.(H)/14 that had returned to Europe. A camera is being fitted in one of the Bf 110s.

March 7, 1942: British Operation *Spotter* off Malta is launched; Spitfires make first appearance in theater

May 26, 1942: Rommel opens major DAK offensive eastward

June 21, 1942: Tobruk falls to Rommel

August 31, 1942: DAK offensive stalls at El Alamein line

September 30, 1942: Luftwaffe ace "Jochen" Marseille is killed bailing out of his new Bf 109 G-2/Trop

October 23, 1942: Montgomery opens massive Eighth Army offensive: second battle of El Alamein develops

November 2, 1942: Operation *Supercharge* breaches Italian–German lines: DAK in full retreat

November 8, 1942: Operation *Torch*, the Allied landings in Morocco and Algeria, commence. Axis forces trapped in pincer

November 15, 1942: Tobruk retaken by the British

November 19, 1942: Benghazi retaken by the British. DAK falls back to Tunisia

1943

February 4, 1943: Remnants of DAK dig in on Mareth Line

February 15, 1943: Battle of Kasserine Pass. Allies suffer 10,000 casualties but retake Kasserine

April 5, 1943: Allies launch Operation *Flax* to sever Axis links between Tunisia and Europe

May 12, 1943: Capture of von Arnim and Messe's surrender a day later—the end of Axis operations in Africa

Introduction: The Italian Offensive

In 1912 Italy had seized Libya from the Ottomans. Following the "March on Rome," Mussolini and his fascists came to power in 1922 with Il Duce's ambition to make the Mediterranean the *Mare Nostro*—"our sea"—as in the Roman *Mare Nostrum*. However, thwarting his ambition, Libya was "stuck" between Tunisia, a French possession, and Egypt, administered by the British, who needed to protect the strategic Suez Canal—the "Route to the Indies."

In 1934, Italian air force Maresciallo Italo Balbo, one of the leading architects of Italian fascism and also known for his pre-war expeditionary flights, was appointed Governor of Libya. Balbo styled himself as the friend of Reichsmarschall Hermann Göring, Commander-in-Chief of the Luftwaffe and Great War ace. He visited him in Germany in 1938 before Göring came to Tripoli in April 1939. The Luftwaffe subsequently mounted shuttle flights between Germany and Tripoli—via Italy—to train its crews on long-range flights.

As international tensions mounted, the colonies of the European powers were at serious risk of being dragged into the mix. While Balbo, Governor General and Commander-in-

In April 1939, Reichsmarschall Hermann Göring was received in Tripoli by Governor Italo Balbo.

At Castel Benito, the Tripoli airfield, Balbo proudly shows off his combat aircraft (S. 81) to the Reichsmarschall. A year later, however, the Italian army in Libya would be incapable of the push toward Cairo.

Chief of Italian North Africa, enjoyed great authority, he was not inclined, in 1940, to take action in Tunisia, which he knew was well defended. He was, however, an ardent advocate of a general offensive against Egypt: he thus came up against the strategic conception of the Italian general staff: a willingness to remain on the defensive.

On May 10, 1940, the Wehrmacht launched its major campaign in the west, inflicting serious reverses on the Franco-British armies. This in turn led Italy to declare war on France and Great Britain a month later. Balbo then insisted on demanding reinforcements, not to defend Libya but to go over to the offensive against Egypt. On June 28, 1940, Marshal Pietro Badoglio sent a telegram to Balbo affirming that he should be ready to invade Egypt on July 15. But Balbo had been killed earlier that same day, victim of a confused Italian antiaircraft battery that had shot down his aircraft, mistaking it for a Royal Air Force (RAF) bomber. General Rodolfo Graziani was then sent urgently to Tripoli, on June 30, having received no directives and even unaware of the telegram fixing July 15 as the date for the launch of the "great offensive" against Egypt. The attack had to be postponed, especially since there was a shortage of 600 to 1,000 vehicles. On September 13, 1940, however, the dice were rolled and the Italian army marched eastward—with little verve. Poorly equipped, lacking in mobility and with low morale, the Italians achieved some initial successes—the capture of Sollum and Sidi Barrani—before suffering a powerful counteroffensive launched by Commonwealth troops who quickly captured Cyrenaica, the eastern territory of Libya.

Arrival of the German Expeditionary Force

With his army on the retreat in both Africa and the Balkans, Mussolini called on his German ally for help. Hitler had little desire to distract his forces—especially since Operation *Barbarossa*, the invasion of the USSR, was in the planning stages. However, he could not allow the RAF to settle in northern Greece and threaten the Romanian oilfields essential for his eastern blitzkrieg. Nor could he allow Tripoli to fall into the hands of the British army probing west out of Egypt. The Luftwaffe was ordered to dispatch what it could to the Mediterranean.

The German X. Fliegerkorps—X Air Corps—assembled a small force of aircraft: Ju 88 and He 111 bombers, and Ju 87 dive-bombers, along with some Bf 110 twins, the only fighter-bombers available. All of them flew into Sicily where they were to be based.

As a long-range strike force, the principal mission for X. Fliegerkorps in the Mediterranean was to hamper enemy forces on the ground in Libya and cut off the flow of supplies to General Archibald Wavell's army. The island of Malta would be key—the Luftwaffe would have to blockade it and subdue it and actively seek out and destroy Royal Navy convoys. While most British shipping came from Gibraltar, sometimes with a stopover in Malta, some of it also transited through the Suez Canal.

A Ju 88 A-5 of 1.(F)/121. This Staffel lost 7A+FH at Benghazi on January 16, 1941.

Luftwaffe strength in the Mediterranean, January 12, 1941

X. Fliegerkorps

1.(F)/121	Ju 88	12 (2)*	Catania
Stab/LG 1	Ju 88	4 (2)	Catania
II./LG 1	Ju 88	38 (38)	Catania
III./LG 1	Ju 88	38 (38)	Catania
II./KG 26	He 111	37 (29)	Comiso
2./KG 4	He 111	12 (12)	Comiso
Stab/St.G 3	Ju 87/He 111	? (8)	Trapani
I./St.G 1	Ju 87	35 (11)	Trapani
II./St.G 2	Ju 87	36 (23)	Trapani

Jafü Sizilien

III./ZG 26	Bf 110	34 (16)	Palermo

* Figures in brackets indicate serviceable aircraft.

The Heinkel He 111 bombers of II./KG 26 were tasked with the first operation mounted by X. Fliegerkorps under Obstlt. Martin Harlinghausen: an attack against a convoy transiting the Suez Canal from the Red Sea, to be launched on January 17, 1941. The day before, the Luftwaffe had lost its first aircraft on African soil when a Ju 88 A-5 of 1.(F)/121 collided with an Italian machine at Benina (Benghazi). The raid flown by II./KG 26 was a disaster. Running into bad weather, strong headwinds and increasingly powerful antiaircraft batteries as they approached the Suez Canal in the dark, the He 111s of the Löwengeschwader—the Lion Squadron—lost 10 of the 12 aircraft committed without even getting close to their targets. Among the missing were the crew of the Kommandeur Helmut Bertram, who was flying his third combat sortie with the Löwengeschwader. The crew of Harlinghausen himself—who as chief of staff had opted to lead the raid—was likewise reported missing. One of the missing airmen managed to return to Italian lines after walking more than 50 kilometers through the desert. A second was rescued by the

The crew of 7A+FH, the first Luftwaffe personnel killed in Africa.

On January 17, 1941, Obstlt. Martin Harlinghausen led the first German raid against the Suez Canal. It proved to be a disaster with 10 aircraft lost.

Italians. Harlinghausen's pilot had put down in the desert after running out of fuel. He and his crew were eventually picked up by another He 111 on a search-and-rescue mission flown by Robert Kowalewski, an experienced aviator who would later be awarded the Knight's Cross and who ended the war at the controls of an Ar 234 jet bomber.

Despite this disastrous experience, the Luftwaffe persevered and II./KG 26 once again launched sorties against Egypt.

On January 29, the He 111s of 2./KG 4 were in turn engaged, departing Comiso with sea mines. The He 111s refueled at Benghazi and then set out on the night of January 30, for Suez where the mines were dropped: three Allied ships were reportedly blown up, temporarily blocking the canal. The Heinkels then landed at Marizza (Rhodes) before returning to Comiso.

On the night of February 3/4, 2./KG 4 was airborne with mines but on this occasion dropped them off Tobruk. However, this did little to curb the Allied advance. On February 6, Benghazi fell to the British, with the Luftwaffe temporarily losing an advance base for its attacks on maritime traffic. Soon afterward, 2./KG 4 flew two more night time mining operations … to Benghazi.

A torpedo-carrying He 111 of II./KG 26. The 'Löwen' or 'Lion' Geschwader specialized in the maritime strike role.

General Erwin Rommel quickly put to use the few aircraft he had at his disposal, such as this Fi 156 Storch which took him back and forth to his frontline units.

The Germans are Coming …

On February 6, 1941, Lieutenant General Erwin Rommel was summoned to appear before the Führer, to take command of the two divisions—one light and one panzer—being sent to Libya. But he also needed aviation resources—close air support and long-range strike capability—to support his ground forces and cover his supply lines. To assist the new Deutsches Afrika Korps (DAK), X. Fliegerkorps in Sicily could only give up 8./ZG 26, the two remaining Staffeln of III./ZG 26 serving in the bomber escort role in the assault on Malta. Ju 52 transports were also active in Africa and, on February 5, it was noted that an airman of KGzbV 9 was wounded in a machine-gun attack on Benina.

On or around January 26, the Ju 87 Stukas of Hptm. Paul-Werner Hozzel's I./St.G. 1 also departed Sicily for Tripoli. Two weeks later, the Stukas were joined by their counterparts from II./St.G. 2 under Major Walter Enneccerus. Like all newcomers to Libya, the airmen soon discovered the particularly inadequate nature of the local facilities.

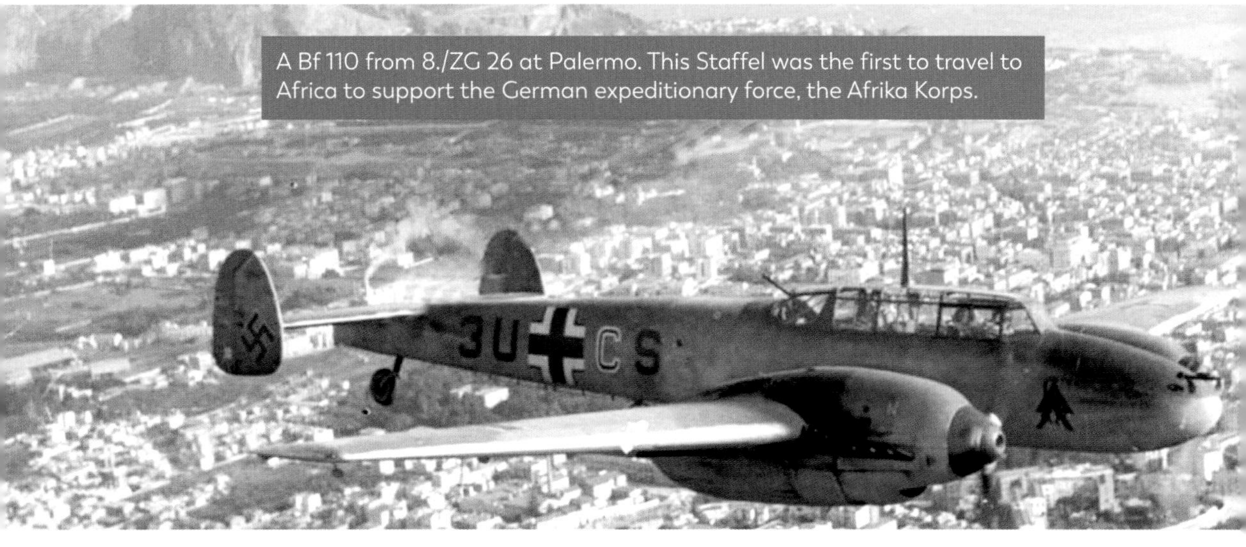

A Bf 110 from 8./ZG 26 at Palermo. This Staffel was the first to travel to Africa to support the German expeditionary force, the Afrika Korps.

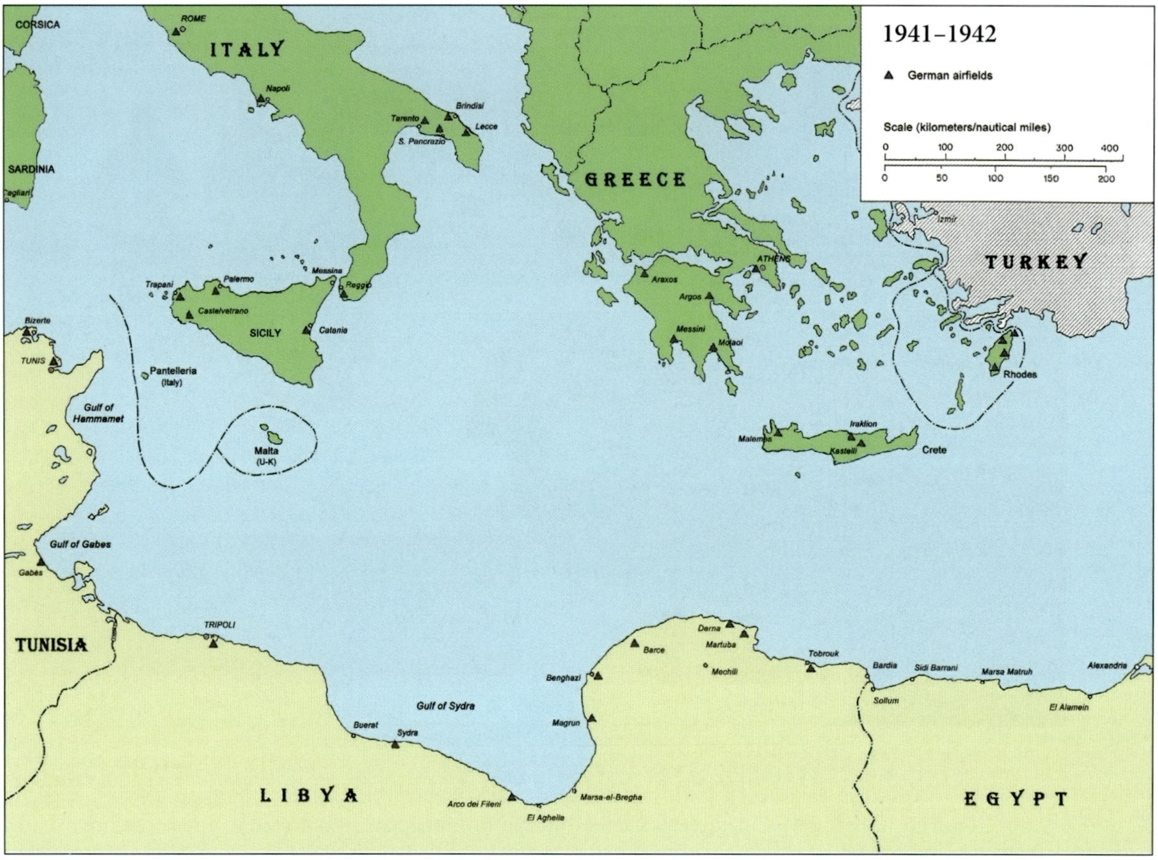

Airfields used by the Luftwaffe in Libya and Egypt.

Airfields used by the Luftwaffe in Tunisia.

First contact for the airmen of III./ZG 26 with African soil. In this press photo, the censor has deleted the 3U code from the fuselage of the Bf 110 twin.

Ju 87 Stukas soon arrived on the African continent.

A Ju 87 Stuka of I./St.G. 1.

German airmen soon experienced the problems associated with war in the desert. The engines of this Bf 110 of the 8./ZG 26 choke in the clouds of sand kicked up by its propellers.

In Cairo, the Afrika Korps was assumed to be on a purely defensive mission to support the few Italian units covering the road to Tripoli. This was not Rommel's vision: he launched everything that could fly as quickly as possible in the face of an RAF weakened by the deployment of most of its aircraft to the Balkans.

As early as February 12—the day of Rommel's arrival in Tripoli—Ju 88s of LG 1 flew their first sorties to Africa from Sicily. Eighteen bombers attacked enemy troops south of Benghazi and a 6. Staffel machine became the unit's first loss on African soil, L1+IP falling to antiaircraft fire.

The next day, February 13, the Bf 110 Staffel from ZG 26, as well as I./St.G. 1 and II./St.G. 2, left for Bir Dufan and, on February 14, all attacked positions at El Agheila, suffering three casualties. The two 8./ZG 26 crew of Bf 110 3U+FR were the first Luftwaffe personnel to be taken captive in Africa.

Meanwhile, also on February 13, 15 Ju 88s of III./LG 1 were airborne from Sicily against the aerodromes and port of Benghazi. LG 1 was then ordered to concentrate on two new *Schwerpünkte* or primary objectives: firstly, targets in the rear of the British lines in North Africa (especially supply routes) and, secondly, escort duties for German convoys shuttling between Italy and Tripoli bringing supplies to the German army in Africa.

Fleets of Ju 52 transports shuttling from Sicily brought in men and equipment to Africa.

A formation of Ju 52s at wavetop height over the Mediterranean.

From Sicily the Ju 88s of III./LG 1 in turn operated over Cyrenaica.

The Luftwaffe's 8.8cm antiaircraft (Flak) guns were pressed into service in the ground role, partly as the army's standard 3.7cm gun could not penetrate the heavy armor of the British Valentine and Matilda tanks.

Luftwaffe strength in the Mediterranean, February 22, 1941

Unit	Aircraft	Strength	Base
X. Fliegerkorps			
1.(F)/121	Ju 88	17 (7)*	Catania
Stab/St.G 3	Ju 87/He 111	5 (2)	Trapani
I./St.G. 1	Ju 87	30 (22)	Trapani
II./Stab St .G 2	Ju 87	38 (31)	Trapani
Stab/LG 1	Ju 88	? (-)	Catania
II./LG 1	Ju 88	24 (13)	Catania
III./LG 1	Ju 88	29 (10)	Catania
II./KG 26	He 111	30 (19)	Comiso
2./KG 4	He 111	9 (7)	Comiso
Jafü Sizilien			
7./JG 26	Bf 109	14 (12)	Gela
1./NJG 3	Bf 110	7 (4)	Gela
8. & 9./ZG 26	Bf 110	40 (31)	Palermo
Fliegerführer Afrika			
7./ZG 26**	Bf 110 (?)		Derna

* Figures in brackets indicate serviceable aircraft.
** Replaced by 8./ZG 26 in Libya during this period.

Rommel Launches His Offensive

On February 14, all serviceable machines of Lehrgeschwader 1 flew sorties in support of the Afrika Korps. The next day, Benghazi was again the target of the Ju 88s of III./LG 1 (one loss). On February 17, British high command assembled its two fighter squadrons at Tobruk. On February 18, they were airborne to intercept a dozen I./St. G. 1 Ju 87s. The following night, the Heinkel He 111s of 2./KG 4 mined the Suez Canal. Several ships reportedly struck mines, blocking all navigation through this key artery for four days.

Lt. Alfred Wehmeyer (center, bareheaded) achieved the inaugural kill returned by ZG 26 in Africa, on February 19, 1941. He was later awarded the Knight's Cross.

Tactical recce Staffel 2.(H)/14 arrived in Libya on February 24. Its Henschel 126s were reassembled after being transferred by ship.

On February 19, the Luftwaffe claimed its first kills in African skies when Bf 110s of 8./ZG 26 escorting II./St.G. 2 Ju 87s to El Agheila shot down two Hurricanes of 3 Squadron Royal Australian Air Force (RAAF). Lt. Wehmeyer's Bf 110 ditched off the coast but the crew was rescued the next day.

On February 24, the air assets available to the DAK received another boost with the arrival in Tripoli of the liaison and short-range reconnaissance Staffel 2.(H)/14, equipped with the Henschel Hs 126. Like III./ZG 26, 2.(H)/14 was very quickly deployed. LG 1 continued its attacks against Allied strongpoints while KG 4 pursued mine-laying activities in the Suez Canal where antiaircraft defenses had been reinforced. II./LG 1 took off from Sicily to lead the first attack mounted by this Gruppe against the fortress of Tobruk. Ack-ack defenses over the target were powerful and one Ju 88 was lost.

II./St.G. 2, operating regularly in Africa, adopted a more appropriate badge for this theater.

"Hajo" Herrmann (center) was a leading bomber pilot and Staffelkäpitan in 7./ KG 30.

In Derna, a Ju 52 has just brought in reinforcements for the Afrika Korps.

February 25 saw the arrival in Sicily from the Netherlands of 7./KG 30 led by its soon-to-be (in)famous Staffelkäpitan Hptm. "Hajo" Hermann—an advance guard of III./KG 30 sent to reinforce X. Fliegerkorps in their fight against the Royal Navy. The next day, the Staffel flew sorties against Malta and, two days later, Africa. The first Ju 88 of the Adlergeschwader was lost over Tobruk on February 28.

To reinforce the much sought-after reconnaissance Ju 88 D aircraft of 1.(F)/121, the Ju 88 and Bf 110 twins of 2.(F)/123 arrived in Catania on March 4. On March 13, 2.(H)/14 suffered its first loss on African soil, one of its Hs 126s the victim of a sandstorm near Zliten (crew killed). Bombing sorties were shared between the two Gruppen of LG 1 operating around Crete and Malta while III./KG 30 would mainly be tasked with missions to Africa.

The transports flew in drums of fuel and crated ordnance.

A Ju 88 of 2.(F)/123. This strategic reconnaissance unit was deployed in the service of the Afrika Korps in March 1941.

Collision on the ground between an Fi 156 and a Hs 126 of 2.(H)/14, possibly the result of a sandstorm.

Discussion at II./St.G. 2 (code T6) before takeoff. At that time, given the weakness of the RAF/SAAF (South African Air Force) fighter force, the Stukas could often operate without significant interference—or losses.

A Ju 88 wearing the insignia of the Adlergeschwader (eagle): the KG 30.

While the RAF was handicapped by its transfers to Greece, Rommel, who had received armor reinforcements, was able to seize the airfield, wells, and fort of El Agheila on March 24. However, the month of March saw only limited clashes in the air as a result of the reduced numbers of aircraft available to both sides. From Comiso, the He 111s of 2./KG 4 and II./KG 26 increased night operations against Alexandria, Suez and the Egyptian ports. Several losses occurred as a result of the strengthening of antiaircraft defenses in Egypt.

Toward Tobruk

On March 27, Rommel was given carte blanche to go over to the offensive while Wavell wrote to Winston Churchill: "The German air attacks on Benghazi have made it impossible for our supply ships to use this port and helped to increase our problems. As a result I lack

Toward mid-April, captured senior officers—Generals Philip Neame, Richard O'Connor, Michael Gambier-Parry, and Brigadier John Combe—were evacuated to Italy in Ju 52 transports. At that time, air links between Italy and Africa were still safe. As usual, the censor masked the codes on the trimotor fuselage.

A Staffel of Ju 87s flying to the east.

tanks in Cyrenaica." After Marsa el Brega on March 31, Agedabia fell on April 2, and the next day the Afrika Korps entered Benghazi. Commonwealth forces were forced to withdraw to Tobruk.

On April 6, 1941 the Germans launched Operation *Marita*, the invasion of the Balkans. Commonwealth troops in Africa, depleted by the headlong offensive against the Italians and calls for reinforcements to be sent to Greece and Crete, now faced a "double" offensive on both sides of the Mediterranean.

While Rommel captured Bardia, Sollom and Capuzzo on April 11, the Axis divisions would encounter the stubborn resistance at the "*Festung Tobruk*" or Fortress Tobruk. Axis losses compelled them to halt the assault, postponing further attacks until the arrival of the 15. Pz.D. and heavy artillery units; Rommel also had to wait until the Luftwaffe, which had contributed so powerfully to the progress of his forces (notably by successfully striking at the enemy's communication lines and vital installations), was able to transfer the remote bases it occupied between Tripoli and Sirte to Marmarica.

Clashes in the air were keenly disputed—although the number of aircraft on both sides was limited. At the beginning of April, I./St.G. 1 was shifted to the Balkans, being replaced by 7. and 8./St.G. 1. Tobruk came under constant air attack and April 14 saw a high number of sorties.

Wounded men on a Ju 52.

The first day fighters in Africa: I./JG 27

Stab I./JG 27
Kommandeur: Hptm Eduard "Edu" Neumann (died August 9, 2004)
Adjudant: Oblt Ludwig Franzisket (RKT, died November 23, 1988)
Lt. Friedrich-Wilhelm Borchert

1./JG 27
Kapitän: Oblt Wolfgang Redlich (RKT, KIA May 29, 1944)
Oblt. Hugo Schneider (KIA January 11, 1942)
Lt. Eugen von Moller
Lt. Hans Remmer (KIA April 2, 1944)
Lt. Werner Schroer (RKT, died February 10, 1985)
Ofw. Gerhard Otto (WIA May 9, 1941)
Ofw. Willy Stephan
Fw. Werner Lange (KIA April 23, 1941)
Fw. Dr Peter Werfft (RKT, died July 23, 1970)
Uffz. Albert Espenlaub (POW December 13, 1941, shot down and KIA February 25, 1942)
Uffz. Heinz Greuel (KIA June 15, 1941)
Uffz. Gerhard Keppler
Uffz. Hans Sippel (KIA April 21, 1941)
Uffz. Günther Steinhausen (RKT, MIA September 6, 1942)

2./JG 27
Kapitän: Hptm. Erich Gerlitz (killed)
Oblt. Ernst Maack (MIA)
Lt. Fritz Keller
Lt. Willi Kothmann (KIA November 2, 1942)
Lt. Erich Schröder (POW May 26, 1941)
Ofhr. Heinrich Pompsch (KIA April 22, 1941)
Ofhr. Hans-Arnold Stahlschmidt (RKT, MIA September 7, 1942)
Ofw. Hermann Förster (POW December 14, 1941)
Fw. Franz Elles (POW December 11, 1941)
Fw. Emil Kaiser
Uffz. Egon Reichstein
Uffz. Rudolf Stöckler (KIA June 15, 1941)

3./JG 27
Kapitän: Oblt. Gerhard Homuth (RKT, KIA August 2, 1943)
Lt. Friedrich Hoffmann (KIA September 15, 1942)
Lt. Karl Kugelbauer (killed July 8, 1942)
Lt. Heinz Schmidt (killed June 28, 1941)
Ofhr. Hans-Joachim Marseille (RKT, died September 30, 1942)
Ofw. Herbert Kowalski (wounded April 9, 1942, transferred?)
Fw. Josef Kraus
Fw. Karl Mentnich
Uffz. Heribert Bauer (died December 25, 1944)
Uffz. Rainer Pöttgen
Gefr. Hermann Köhne (WIA May 1, 1941)

Carrying a drop tank, this Bf 109 E of I./JG 27 is airborne from Sicily en route to Libya

In mid-April, a much-anticipated fighter backup arrived in Africa as the "Emils" of I./JG 27 commanded by Hptm. "Edu" Neumann, a veteran of the Condor Legion, reached the North African theater. Having participated in the battles of France and Britain, the Gruppe already had a number of aces in its ranks and was to become synonymous with the DAK and the campaign in the Western Desert. Up to this point the only fighters available to Rommel were Bf 110 twins. The Bf 109s of I./JG 27 displayed the Gruppe emblem: a map of Africa surmounted with a leopard and the head of a native African that dated to the formation of the unit under its first commander, Hptm. Helmut Riegel, who hailed from one of Germany's African colonies. Initially, the pilots flew from Ain el Gazala, a more or less flat and stony area with no facilities or comforts.

On April 18, 8./LG 1, under Oblt. Hermann Hogeback, left Catania for Benina airfield (Benghazi). The next day I./JG 27 was engaged for the first time in combat in Africa. Two Hurricanes were shot down. Shortly afterward, following another encounter, Lt. Schroer escaped unscathed from a forced landing in the desert. The first JG 27 dogfights were positive: two kills for one loss. On April 20, 1941, I./KGzbV 9 lost two Ju 52s shot down by fighters near Benghazi.

Following their arrival on African soil, the pilots of I./JG 27 discuss upcoming sorties.

On April 21, over Tobruk, Ofw. Espenlaub (1./JG 27) returned his first kill. But I./JG 27 lost Uffz. Sippel, the first from Gruppe Neumann brought down on African soil. 8./LG 1 departed Benghazi for Derna. On April 22, Tobruk was under constant pressure. In an early afternoon dogfight the talented Ofhr. Hans-Joachim Marseille (3./JG 27) returned his eighth kill shortly before being shot down himself—this was the day of his first kill in Libyan skies and he was perhaps fortunate to escape unharmed. Fighting over Tobruk remained fierce. On April 27, F/O Arthur Weller (274 Squadron) carried out a risky, long-range sortie to strafe Benina airfield, destroying four KGzbV 104 Ju 52s.

Renewed Assault by the Axis, May 1941

On April 30, the Axis army resumed their assault on Tobruk. Preceded by an intense Stuka attack, the assault troops overran the Australian front lines but, despite some heavy fighting, the Germans had to settle for occupying Ras el Madouer and, on May 2, the attack was stopped, Rommel deciding to bypass and isolate the port. Tobruk famously remained under siege.

On May 1, 3./JG 27 was active over the town fortress. Ofhr. Marseille claimed two Hurricanes shot down as did Oblt. Homuth. On May 2, at least four 8./ZG 26 Bf 110s succumbed to antiaircraft fire over Tobruk. After the cessation of fighting for Tobruk, there was a lull as strength was rebuilt.

On the night of May 7/8, II./KG 26 was heavily engaged over Suez, losing no fewer than four He 111 H-5 bombers on this objective. The minelayers of 2./KG 4 supporting the Löwengeschwader described this mission as a "success."

On May 10, the Oberkommando der Wehrmacht (OKW), the High Command of the Wehrmacht, launched Operation *Merkur*, the airborne invasion of Crete. RAF units based in North Africa were again obliged to reorganize and divide up their meagre forces.

LG 1 pilot Lt. Gerd Stamp in front of his Ju 88. Stamp would be awarded the Knight's Cross for his audacious attacks on British shipping in the Med.

The Bf 109s of I./JG 27 shot down large numbers of Hurricanes and P-40s during this period.

British Counterattacks Fail

While Axis forces were stalling in front of Tobruk, General Wavell was preparing a counteroffensive to take advantage of an influx of reinforcements. This was to be the first in a series of localized British counteroffensives over the following weeks. The air forces on both sides were to play key roles in the actions.

Operation *Brevity*

On May 16, RAF and SAAF aircraft were dispatched to machine-gun German positions and enemy columns. On the morning of May 21, 14 Squadron launched its Blenheims against the Capuzzo–Tobruk road. This first mission turned to tragedy as the RAF twin-engines were surprised by 3./JG 27, the Bf 109s claiming five shot down. On a subsequent sortie Ofhr. Marseille was once again forced to belly-land in the desert with his engine hit.

Over the following days, the RAF intervened increasingly over Crete, leaving free rein to the Ju 87s in the desert. On May 25, 2./KG 4 began its return to its Dutch base in Soesterberg and left the Mediterranean after having flown two final mining missions over Malta. The actions targeting the Suez Canal would now be left solely to II./KG 26.

Although the fighting in Crete attracted the most attention, a number of Blenheims continued their desert raids. On May 31, Crete fell to the Germans. The surviving Blenheims were brought back while 272 Squadron (Beaufighters) entered the fray, taking up a role similar to that of the Bf 110 *Zerstörer* (heavy fighter, lit. "destroyer") in the desert: ground support, shipping escort and long-range strike missions.

Given the evolution of the conflict in North Africa, the Allied air forces were strengthened, but on June 8, the invasion of Syria resulted in several RAF squadrons, including the Beaufighter squadron, relocating to Palestine. On June 10, F/O Hamlyn of 250 Squadron shot down a Ju 88 of 2.(F)/123 over Alexandria (crew missing). This is the first mention of this reconnaissance Staffel in more than two months. During this time, 2.(F)/123 was widely deployed in Greece during Operation *Merkur*.

Operation *Battleaxe*

The strengthening of the RAF/SAAF was due to the preparation of a more powerful operation than *Brevity*, this time aimed at destroying the German army corps by engaging six fighter squadrons, four medium bomber squadrons and four heavy bomber squadrons. Launched on June 15, *Battleaxe* seemed to get off to a good start. But the element of surprise was lost as the previous day Luftwaffe reconnaissance aircraft had informed Rommel that a major British action was imminent, allowing the "Desert Fox" to maneuver his two armored divisions. The offensive then deteriorated into a series of small engagements. By the morning of June 17, a British defeat was complete. Wavell, after reviewing the situation, approved the decision to retreat. Running out of fuel, Rommel could not exploit his victory and could not hope to reach Egypt. However, this latest DAK victory greatly impressed Berlin and Rome. However, leaving the fortress town of Tobruk under siege and pushing on as far as his depleted force allowed him was a mistake that would take Rommel over a year to rectify.

While *Battleaxe* lasted only a few days, in the air dogfighting was fierce and lasted more than a week. Faced with a reinforced RAF/SAAF presence, the German fighters received only a minor contribution: a detachment of 7./JG 26 from Sicily which had been operating for weeks over Malta. On June 14, led by their Kapitän, Joachim Müncheberg, the airmen of 7./JG 26 reached Ain el Gazala where the unit was placed under the operational control of I./JG 27. In the early hours of the same day five aircraft from 1 Squadron SAAF were

A Bf 109 E from 7./JG 26 near a Bf 110 from 9./ZG 26. The Emils (not equipped with engine filters) were initially serviced by I./JG 27 personnel but suffered from the effects of the sand.

On June 14, 1 Squadron SAAF's Capt Driver was shot down by another ace, Oblt. Franzisket. Taken captive, he was "entertained" by his captor..

escorting a Maryland in a raid on Gazala. Captain Ken Driver, a 10-kill ace, found himself alone to defend the bomber. Oblt. Franzisket (3./JG 27), who had been scrambled from Gazala, shot down both the fighter and bomber. Driver was captured and "entertained" at I./JG 27. He was shown over Franzisket's aircraft and the two aces held a long discussion about tactics before the South African departed for captivity.

The Hs 126s of 2.(H)/14, widely used to monitor the advance of the opposing columns, lost two aircraft to Allied fighters. An Hs 126 was destroyed (crew unharmed) and the first Bf 110 of the Staffel was shot down near El Halfaya (crew captured). Gradually, the Messerschmitt 110 would replace the Hs 126 and Fi 156 in 2.(H)/14.

The next day, June 15, 274 Squadron RAF was airborne very early, claiming a Fiat CR.42, a Regia Aeronautica machine absent from the front for some time (except Luftwaffe aircraft escort duty). The fighting was non-stop throughout the day. Ofhr. Hans-Arnold Stahlschmidt was credited with the first in his long series of kills while his comrade Lt. Friedrich Hoffmann was also credited with a Hurricane. On June 16, the British continued their advance toward Sollom. Over Sollom, a Ju 87 of II./St. G. 2 fell victim to enemy ack-ack while fighters were lost on both sides.

2.(H)/14 (code 5F) gradually replaced its Hs 126s with Bf 110s. On June 14, the first 110 was lost over El Halfaya.

A Kittyhawk shot down in the desert. Allied fighters would suffer at the hands of the Bf 109 pilots of I./JG 27.

On June 17, British ground forces withdrew while the opposing air forces were in almost constant action. Seven aircraft from 1 Squadron SAAF were surprised by eight Bf 109s—a mixed formation from I./JG 27 and 7./JG 26—that shot down three Hurricanes. Oblt Klaus Mietusch of the latter Staffel was credited with his 10th kill. Ofhr. Hans-Joachim Marseille added to his scoreboard. On June 18, several Tomahawks of 250 Squadron were lost. During a machine-gun attack on the Capuzzo–Tobruk–El Adem road, one RAF fighter was shot down by Flak and three others by 1./JG 27. It was on this note that the British offensive ended and a quieter period began, lasting several weeks.

Lull

Following the two British setbacks, leadership was subsequently assumed by General Claude Auchinleck. On the Axis side, at a meeting held on June 2 at the Brenner Pass, it was decided that Tobruk—as key to DAK supply lines—should be captured as soon as possible to enable artillery, armor, and fuel to be shipped into Libya. The chief Axis issues from the outset were thus primarily logistical. The weeks following the end of *Battleaxe* saw only skirmishes on the ground with mediocre gains. In the air, fighting continued, less vigorously, with Tobruk remaining the *Schwerpunkt* of air activity.

On June 22, 1941, *Barbarossa*, the invasion of Soviet Russia, was launched. This vast operation naturally impacted German activity in the Mediterranean sector. On June 23, Ultra revealed the number of single-engined fighter aircraft present in Africa: I./JG 27 had 26 airworthy machines out of 35, while 7. /JG 26 had only six serviceable. The Müncheberg Staffel had been transferred to Greece but, as I./JG 27 had insufficient numbers against a numerically superior RAF, 7./JG 26 returned to Ain el Gazala on the 27th. On June 23, an He 111 H-5 of II./KG 26 ditched at sea off Alexandria after a raid on Egypt (one survivor). The half

An He 111 from KG 26. Although based outside Africa, these aircraft flew sorties in support of the Afrika Korps, often to Egypt.

Units under operational control of Fliegerführer Afrika, June 21, 1941

2.(H)/14	Hs 126/Bf 110	18 (13)	Libya
2.(F)/123	Ju 88, Bf 110	7 (2)	Tatoi
7./JG 26	Bf 109	17 (13)	Ain el Gazala
I./JG 27	Bf 109	34 (25)	Ain el Gazala
III./ZG 26	Bf 110	25 (22)	Derna
I./St.G 1	Ju 87	25 (21)	Tmimi
II./St.G 2	Ju 87	27 (27)	Tmimi
III./LG 1	Ju 88	27 (11)	Derna

* Figures in brackets indicate serviceable aircraft.

During this period 1.(F)/121 was on leave in Germany.

dozen Bf 109s of 7./JG 26 resumed their missions and Staka (Staffelkapitän) Müncheberg was credited with his 45th kill—a Hurricane of 6 Squadron—on June 24. For its part, I./JG 27 continued its escort and patrol duties, claiming a number of kills.

The German day fighter force—*der Tagjagd*—also suffered a number of reverses. June 28 saw the disappearance over Capuzzo of Lt. Heinz Schmidt, a 3./JG 27 ace. In addition, three Bf 109s of I./JG 27 were seriously damaged.

Two days later, on June 30, a maritime convoy steaming off Tobruk and covered by 73 and 250 Squadron aircraft was the target for Stukas escorted by a force of Fiat G.50s, Bf 110s and Bf 109s. A Stuka of II./St. G. 2 was damaged and two Bf 110s of 8./ZG 26 were lost. Two Hurricanes were shot down. On the same day, another attack on a convoy led to further losses that were so severe that 6 Squadron was withdrawn from operations on July 1, taking advantage of the slowdown in fighting.

However, ground-attack missions continued on both sides. On July 4, a 1./St.G. 1 Ju 87 was brought down by ack-ack over Tobruk. On July 7, six Hurricanes of 73 Squadron took off to shoot up the airfields of Sidi Azeiz and Gambut. Only one would return to base.

Oblt. Joachim Müncheberg, leading 7./JG 26, was prominent in the Mediterranean but his unit would only remain there for a short time. Here he greets General Rommel who is on a flying visit in his personal He 111.

A bombing raid underway over Tobruk.

In the absence of 1.(F)/121 on leave in the Reich, 2.(F)/123 was widely deployed on reconnaissance sorties. On July 9, a Ju 88 of this Staffel crashed on takeoff from Derna aerodrome. Three days later, a Ju 88 A-5 was intercepted over Egypt by two Hurricanes of 30 and 33 Squadrons airborne from El Amryia, near Alexandria. From an altitude of 7,900 meters, the German pilot threw his machine into a dive but he was nevertheless caught and F/Lt Vernon Woodward dispatched him with a short burst that sent the Junkers crashing into the desert.

On July 15, there was a major aerial clash near Tobruk. 73 and 229 Squadrons were flying a patrol over a small group of vessels off the fortress town when they encountered a formation of Ju 87s of II./St. G. 2, protected by Bf 110s of 8. /ZG 26 and some Bf 109s. Six Stukas and one Bf 110 were claimed. Staffelkapitän Müncheberg (7./JG 26) was credited with his 46th kill. Ofw. Richard Heller (8./ZG 26) desperately attempted to hold off more than 10 enemy fighters to protect the Ju 87s, a feat cited in the award of his Knight's Cross. Heller claimed three Curtiss P-40s and his machine-gunner, Uffz. Heinz Bövers, a fourth. As usual, kills were hard to ascertain with accuracy. Thus, the six Ju 87s brought down proved to be "only" three and only two Hurricanes went down.

At that time, I./JG 27 received several debutant pilots as reinforcements to fill the unit's serious losses of six killed, one POW and one seriously wounded. One of them was the young Ofhr. Friedrich Körner. Arriving straight from fighter training school, he was posted

Ofw. Richard Heller (8./ZG 26) earned the Knight's Cross for his feats of arms in North Africa. He is seen here with his regular BF (radio operator) Ofw Heinz Bövers.

Oblt. Otto Heymer led the Hs 126-equipped 2.(H)/14 and the first battlefield reconnaissance Staffel serving with the Afrika Korps. He received the Knight's Cross for the good performance of his unit but left Africa in August 1941. He was killed in Russia in 1943.

to 2./JG 27 and seems to have been very quickly fascinated by the increasing notoriety of his new comrade—and possibly role model—H-J. Marseille. Körner would in turn become one of the greatest German aces in the desert.

RAF reinforcements continued to arrive in theater and new machines such as the Martlet, the British version of the American Grumman F4F Wildcat, appeared in the desert. The month of August began with a clash between 1 Squadron SAAF and Ju 87s during a maritime patrol near Sidi Barrani. Four Ju 87s were claimed but only two Ju 87 R-2s of I./St.G. 1 were in actual fact lost with their crews. Three South African airmen failed to return. 1./JG 27 filed four claims.

As the fighters got to grips with each other, the bombers' actions continued. On August 3, an 8./LG 1 aircraft crashed on takeoff from Derna. On the night of August 4, during a major assault on Ismailia, an He 111 from 5./KG 26 was lost. In addition, two Ju 88 A-5s of 1./LG 1 failed to return. One was shot down by a nightfighter (crew killed), the other was hit by an AA shell (crew captured). The following night, an LG 1 aircraft returning from an attack in Egypt was the victim of an instrument failure, and got lost, landing near Fetyie in neutral Turkey. The crew was interned until the end of 1941 before returning to the unit. On the night of August 7/8, 1./LG 1 lost its Kapitän when his Ju 88 was targeted by an antiaircraft battery shortly after dropping its bombs on Alexandria. The twin-engined aircraft was probably finished off by a nightfighter—possibly a 30 Squadron machine—and the pilot and one of his comrades, the only survivors from the crew, bailed out and were captured.

On August 9, a notable encounter took place over the sea when a 230 Squadron Sunderland was caught up in dogfight with a Dornier 24 of 7. Seenotstaffel. The fight apparently ended in a draw.

A Bf 110 from 1./NJG 3 in the Mediterranean. Despite its camouflage, this unit's main task was not to engage the RAF's Wellington bombers at night but to support III./ZG 26 Bf 110s by day due to the shortage of *Zerstörer* aircraft.

Obstlt. Walter Sigel, Kommodore of St. G. 3, received the Oak Leaves to the Knight's Cross in September 1942 in recognition of his unit's successes.

Around this time, the Stab/St.G. 3 under Obstlt. Walter Sigel arrived from Greece to head up the two Stuka Gruppen operating in Africa: I./St.G. 1 (Derna) and II./St.G. 2 (Tmimi). On August 10, a 451 Squadron pilot shot down near Bardia the Hs 126 of 2.(H)/14 flown by the unit's Kapitän, Oblt. Otto Heymer. The presence of the Staffelkapitän over the front line was hardly a surprise to his men since Heymer seems to have been something of a dare-devil. Nevertheless, a few days later, Heymer would give up his command as Kapitän. On August 11, 2 SAAF Squadron claimed a *Zerstörer*. It was not in fact a Bf 110 of III./ZG 26 but a nightfighter of 1./NJG 3 (Hptm. Erhard Peters) recently arrived in Derna from Greece.

On August 13, 2.(F)/123 took advantage of the return from leave of 1.(F)/121 to depart for Germany, only returning at the end of September. The other *Aufklärer*, or reconnaissance, units continued their missions, which had quickly become key.

Throughout this period, LG 1 pursued operations against Allied shipping. On the night of August 22/23, six III./LG 1 Ju 88s successfully raided Tobruk harbor. But other twins encountered P-40s during an attack on a convoy near Sidi Barrani and lost one machine (a sole survivor). Throughout this period, Lehrgeschwader 1 was continuously in action against enemy installations and shipping. On August 25, I. and II./LG 1, based in Eleusis, mined the port of Tobruk. On the night of August 25/26, six Ju 88s from these two Gruppen attacked the port facilities of Alexandria. On the night of August 27/28, five Ju 88s were aloft over Suez, setting fire to oil tanks in Port Taufiq. Meanwhile, III./LG 1, based in Derna, continued its so-called *bewaffnete Aufklärungen*—armed reconnaissance sorties. On the night of August 28/29, II./LG 1 concentrated on the Mersa Matruh equipment depot but lost a Ju 88 A-5.

In early September, there was a twofold increase in aerial activity. According to Karl Gundelach, "the bombers of 10th Air Corps had largely failed, over the preceding months, to achieve any sort of clear success in their attacks on the ports of the Nile Delta." This was partly due to the fact that 6./KG 26 did not have enough adequate torpedoes. In late August, the Ob.d.L.—Luftwaffe High Command—temporarily dispatched I./KG 40 to the Med-iterranean, the Gruppe departing the French Atlantic coast for Greece.

To compensate for the lack of bombers operating against Egypt and the Suez Canal, the Luftwaffe transferred elements of I./KG 40 from France, including several Fw 200 Condors.

The KG 40 Fw 200 Condors, shuttling between Europe and Africa, also transported POWs to Europe, such as these Indian soldiers.

This detachment took with them six four-engined Fw 200 Condors and nine He 111s. Their crews were torpedo-attack specialists. The long-range Condors operated from Eleusis near Athens or Derna to attack the southern sector of the Gulf of Suez while the He 111s, based in Heraklion, Crete, could reach Suez harbor. On September 2, 12 LG 1 bombers targeted ships in Port Said. This was the starting point of an uninterrupted series of night attacks that lasted until September 10 and saw Port Said bombed, but also the Straits of Suez and Alexandria, as well as shipping in the Gulf of Suez, the Dead Sea and the northern sector of the Red Sea. On September 16 and 17, aircraft even ranged over the airfields at Heliopolis and Abukir. I./KG 40 aircraft would eventually repatriate combatants and Italian settlers to Europe. On the nights of September 7, 10, and 12, LG 1 lost four Ju 88s during these attacks on Egypt.

While the bomber offensive was growing, so was the strength of the fighter force. The RAF had to evacuate Sidi Barrani in the face of losses over this sector. For example, September 14 was an important day of activity. At about 1600 hours, a Rotte (a pair, or a raft) of 1./JG 27 intercepted a formation of two aircraft from 451 Squadron. Lt. Schroer and Fw. Oswald gave the two reconnaissance pilots no chance. Shortly afterward, 33 Squadron was escorting Marylands from 24 Squadron SAAF to bomb panzer concentrations, for the second time that day. 3/JG 27 reacted vigorously and Oblt. Homuth returned his 24th kill, a bomber that exploded in mid-air. Homuth then shot down a Hurricane, as did Lt. Marseille (18th LS) and Hoffmann (7th LS). Finally, at around 6:30 p.m., five P-40s of 3 Squadron RAAF left Gambut and ran into 1./JG 27. Oblt. Redlich and Uffz. Steinhausen returned their 23rd and sixth kills respectively.

Ofhr. Marseille seen inspecting one of his victims, a Hurricane.

On September 18, 1941, the entente between Axis airmen was again undermined when Italian naval gunners shot down air-sea rescue Dornier 24 KK+UL.

Reinforcements for the *Tagjagd*

On September 18, Italian naval antiaircraft fire shot down Dornier 24 KK+UL (WNr 7) of 7. Seenotstaffel. Assigned to the forward base in the Gulf of Bunbah (Seenot Tripolis), it was the second Do 24 lost in the Mediterranean. Three airmen died in this unfortunate "friendly fire" incident.

On September 22, 1941, the advance elements of a major Luftwaffe fighter reinforcement arrived: II./JG 27. This Gruppe had been deployed for barely a month over the northern sector of the new Eastern Front before being withdrawn on July 24. Led by Hptm. Wolfgang Lippert, II./JG 27 had returned to Döberitz where the pilots converted to the more modern Bf 109 F-4. Members of the unit had also received tropical equipment and were vaccinated against various diseases found in the Mediterranean area. This arrival allowed 7./JG 26, which had failed to achieve much over the preceding weeks, to be freed up. Aircraft were, however, largely unserviceable, having not been fitted with sand filters. The DB 601N engine had proved completely unsuitable for war in the desert and, on September 24, 7./JG 26 departed Africa.

The first sorties flown by II./JG 27 (4. Staffel) took place on September 26, in the Sollum sector but were uneventful except for 30-percent damage sustained by a Bf 109 F-4 on landing at Gazala.

The new arrivals were thus assigned to I./St.G. 3, a new Stuka unit operating in support of the Afrika Korps. The date the Stukas arrived in Africa is not known with certainty, but

On September 22, II./JG 27 arrived in Libya equipped with the Bf 109 F fitted with sand filters. Its pilots would very quickly see action.

One notable II./JG 27 pilot was Ofw. Otto Schulz from 4. Staffel. He would quickly carve out a reputation in the desert.

Briefing at 2.(H)/14. Note the officer's white cap, authorized in the Mediterranean (and in some other theaters) during the summer months.

A Ju 52 of KGzbV 1 (wearing the insignia of the bear of Berlin) has just unloaded its passengers, new reinforcements for the Afrika Korps.

In Profile:
Reconnaissance aircraft

Hs 126 of 2.(H)/14.
The first insignia of that unit, an edelweiss, was totally inappropriate for that theater of war.

the Gruppe likely made the journey shortly after the appointment of its Kommandeur Sigel as coordinator of the two Stuka Gruppen already present in Africa. I./St.G. 3 had taken an active part in the fighting in the Balkans and Crete and it almost certainly required several weeks to return to fighting strength. An organization chart of the time lists it under X. Fliegerkorps control. Was I./St.G. 3 then "loaned" to the Fliegerführer Afrika? This strengthening was explained by the fact that, contrary to Axis hopes, the fortress town of Tobruk had not capitulated during September and more sustained pressure would have to be exerted to achieve this result.

On October 1, 1 Squadron SAAF began replacing its P-40s with Hurricanes. Two days later, II./JG 27 opened its African scoreboard. In the morning, 5. Staffel Friedrichs caught by surprise half a dozen 33 Squadron Hurricanes from Buq Buq engaged in escorting a 451 Squadron reconnaissance aircraft. Sgt Lowry would be Uffz. Horst Reuter's second kill. The British pilot jumped clear before his machine exploded. In the afternoon, it was the turn of 4./JG 27 to intercept a similar formation—given the high losses of the 451st, its aircraft were now to be heavily escorted—near Sidi Barrani. This time, in addition to close protection provided by the 33rd, the Hurricanes had an additional escort of 112 Squadron aircraft. It was a pilot of this last squadron, Sgt Stirrat, who was the victim of 4./JG 27's attack: two pilots, Oblt Rödel and Lt Arthur Schacht, were credited with a *Luftsieg* (air victory, or kill). Another Hurricane was lost that day over Tripoli. But this reconnaissance aircraft assigned to 2 PRU was downed by the Italians. 2.(F)/123 flew its first sortie since its return from Germany that day, a flight over Sidi Barrani.

Two Ju 87s of 3./St.G.1 displaying the unit's crow emblem.

On October 7, II./JG 27 lost its first pilot over Africa when, in an early morning clash with three Marylands from 12 Squadron SAAF, Lt. Gustav-Adolf Langanke was shot down and killed by defensive fire from a South African machine-gunner. Langanke was an ace with seven kills (the first over London and the other six in Russia). He was probably surprised by the tactics employed on this front, which were very different from those he had known up to that point. On the same day, a Ju 87 of I./St.G. 1 crashed and exploded near Tmimi (the crew were able to bail out in time). The three Gruppen of Ju 87s continued their missions without interruption—missions so numerous it is impossible to list them or even provide an outline here.

Commonwealth units continued to be strengthened. On October 9, a new unit equipped with Curtiss P-40s arrived in the desert—4 Squadron SAAF. On the 14th, Allied air forces in the desert regrouped to prepare for the upcoming offensive. It would take place a month later.

On October 17, II./JG 27 suffered a second loss when Oblt. Franz Schultz (6. /JG 27) was killed by antiaircraft fire, probably during a strafing sortie over the Sollum–Sidi Barrani sector. He was reported missing. Throughout this period 1./JG 27 was temporarily absent from the North African theater, having been the first I./JG 27 Staffel to be recalled home, to convert to the more modern Bf 109 "Friedrich."

At the same time the RAF targeted Luftwaffe and Italian aerodromes. On October 18, six Blenheims attacked Gazala, wounding I./JG 27 personnel. Barbed wire was dropped with the bombs in an attempt to puncture enemy aircraft tires on takeoff. However, ground staff took to simply raking the ground to remove these "English porcupines," as this new but ineffective weapon was dubbed.

During this period 80 Squadron RAF joined the Libyan front flying "Hurribombers"—capable of carrying eight 40lb bombs—and was tasked with supporting ground troops. For its part, 274 Squadron replaced its old Hurricane Mk I fighters with the more modern Mk II. The RAF was progressively building its strength in anticipation of a forthcoming offensive against the Afrika Korps. On October 25, 260 Squadron, equipped with Hurricanes, arrived from Palestine; four days later, it was the turn of 94 Squadron, also equipped with Hurricanes. In addition, 33 Squadron was starting to receive the long-range Mk I. The Luftwaffe was

Lt. Hans Sehringer of 2.(F)/123 almost died on October 25, 1941 when his Bf 110 crashed while returning from a sortie against Alexandria. However, he returned to combat and was awarded the Knight's Cross in December 1942.

Flying over an oasis is a Bf 110 from 8./ZG 26. This Staffel took part in the bold but unsuccessful action against Giarabub on November 15, 1941.

now facing a much-reinforced RAF/RAAF/SAAF.

Also on the 25th, Bf 110 E-3 4U+XK of 2. (F)/123 returning from a mission to Alexandria, was victim of an engine problem. Its pilot, Lt. Hans Sehringer, could not reach Crete or Sicily and was forced to crash-land at Derna. His radio operator, Uffz. Hans Sölter (who had just celebrated his 100th combat sortie) was killed instantly. The pilot remained unconscious in the wreckage, which caught fire. A member of the ground crew, Uffz. Künzer, then braved the fire to pull Sehringer out of his machine. After a field hospital stay, the pilot returned to combat operations and went on to receive the Knight's Cross.

On November 1, nine Marylands from 21 Squadron SAAF bombed Derna. Five Stukas of I./St.G. 1 were hit on the ground and at least three were destroyed. Three twin-engined Italian aircraft were also damaged. On the 2nd, another Ju 87—this time from I./St.G. 3—was destroyed near Amalas. The aircraft was likely the victim of a technical problem and here one of the crew survived.

On the 4th, a contest of no consequence took place over Bir Tengeder between a Bf 109 F and a Maryland of 223 Squadron—although the latter's machine-gunners claimed the fighter as "destroyed." Various clashes between the RAF/SAAF and Regia Aeronautica occurred over the next few days. At that time, the Italians had deployed Macchi C.202 fighters which were far superior to the Fiat CR.42, with the result that dogfights became more keenly contested.

On November 7, a Ju 88 of 2.(F)/123 was machine-gunned by an MC.200 near Derna, the trigger-happy Italian pilot unleashing several bursts that killed two of the hapless German crew (the radio operator and the observer), causing some damage to the unfortunate German twin.

Around this period, the RAF received four B-17s. These American machines had not yet had their teething problems entirely ironed out. Assigned to 220 Squadron, they

The Fi 156 Storch was a useful liaison machine in the desert.

During an inspection, I./JG 27 crews stand to attention in front of their Bf 109 Emils.

operated at night alongside the Wellingtons. Although the Axis night defenses were weak—and I./NJG 3 had left the Mediterranean at the beginning of the month—the four-engined aircraft hardly distinguished themselves at the outset. On the 8th, the first daylight raid was mounted by two of these "Flying Fortresses"—though not yet known by this nickname—in the Tobruk area to relieve enemy pressure against the fortress. One aircraft was forced to land behind enemy lines due to engine trouble. The crew was able to scuttle the aircraft before returning to their own lines the next day. In a second raid, a B-17 was briefly attacked by Bf 109 Fs.

Attacked on their own airfields, the Luftwaffe decided to strike back. An operation targeting a former Italian, British-held airfield at the remote oasis of Giarabub was launched on November 15, the Luftwaffe putting up six 8./ZG 26 Bf 110s and nine Ju 88s of III./LG 1 for the mission. Rather than heavy fighters, the *Zerstörer* operated as light bombers carrying small S.D. anti-personnel bombs. Bf 109s of JG 27, equipped like the Bf 110s, with drop tanks, were also deployed. However, the hastily launched operation meant that these three forces flew independently. Returning from the strike, the Staffelkapitän of 8./ZG 26, Oblt. Fritz Schulze-Dickow, had to put down in the desert, his 110 having been damaged by ground fire. He was recovered with his machine-gunner by Ofw. Hans Swoboda who

An 8.8cm gun defending an airfield. Flak personnel regularly suffered severe casualties during the large-scale RAF/SAAF bombing raids.

In case of a forced landing in the desert, this Ju 87 crew carried an impressive amount of firearms and survival equipment.

landed nearby. A Ju 88 also had to land in the desert on the return flight; the crew was unharmed and the aircraft was recovered. Two other bombers returned to land at Benina with damage assessed at 30 percent. German propaganda reported that "twenty-two aircraft were destroyed on the ground." In fact, one Blenheim was destroyed, with five other bombers and two Hurricanes damaged. A handful of Hurricane aircraft that had been able to scramble clashed with the JG 27 fighters that arrived late on the scene, one Hurricane being shot down by Ofw. Albert Espenlaub while a second made a forced landing. The raid on Giarabub enjoyed mixed results and was only notable for the distances covered. Having caught the oasis garrison unawares, the Luftwaffe lost one Bf 110 for the destruction of three aircraft and seven others damaged: small return for the effort expended. There was little chance that this ambitious raid would be repeated.

On November 16, Special Air Service (SAS) troops under command of Captain David Stirling emplaned to five 216 Squadron Bombay transports to attack Axis aerodromes. The lead aircraft, with commando Captain Thompson on board, then got lost and was forced to land. The next day, the commandos on board discovered that they were close to Gazala airfield and captured a lone Italian soldier who had unwisely come to inspect their machine. The aircraft took off again but was then attacked by a Rotte of Bf 109s that had been scrambled. Ofw. Otto Schulz (4./JG 27) shot down the Bombay at an altitude of about 50 meters. The survivors were captured and taken to a German airfield where they were greeted by Kommandeur Lippert. The story did not end there for Thompson. Given his rank and seniority, the commando officer was put in an Fi 156 to be taken to the rear. However, the Storch had to land in the desert due to a technical problem and the pilot went off to seek help, leaving his prisoner in the care of the second passenger, a meteorologist. Taking advantage of the opportunity, Thompson knocked out his unfortunate makeshift guard and fled. However, he came across the crew of a Ju 52 that had also been forced to land. He was recaptured and, later that evening, shared a drink with the meteorologist, who evidently bore no grudge.

The next day, the British launched Operation *Crusader*.

The weapons would be used, if necessary, to kill gazelles for food but also to repel belligerent Bedouins.

The desert war became a contest of resourcefulness on both sides. Anything that could be recovered would be put to use, such as this ex-British Bedford truck attached to I./JG 27.

| Operation *Crusader*

On November 18, 1941 Claude Auchinleck launched the Eighth Army on the ambitious Operation *Crusader*, the principal objective being to lift the siege of Tobruk. Counted in the ranks of the Eighth Army—118,000 men in all—were Britons, Indians, Australians, New Zealanders, South Africans, Poles, and Czechs. Facing them was Rommel's 119,000-strong Afrika Korps. The Allied inventory included 738 tanks and 724 aircraft (616 serviceable), while the Axis forces had around 400 panzers and 536 aircraft (342 serviceable) on its books.

The Luftwaffe Shortly Before *Crusader*

Despite the failure of the British army's two assaults, the Axis army in Africa had not by any stretch of the imagination decided the outcome. In early 1941, X. Fliegerkorps based in Sicily had only very small numbers of personnel and, to support General Rommel's offensive, this air corps had been forced to second to Africa the Bf 110s from III./ZG 26 and the Ju 87s from I./St.G. 1 and II./St.G. 2: Ju 88s of LG 1 were also based in Libya while II./KG 26 and 2./KG 4 were engaged from Sicily against the Suez Canal and Egypt.

To meet the Afrika Korps' strategic reconnaissance needs, 1.(F)/121 and 2.(F)/123 operated over Libya and, for tactical reconnaissance, the Hs 126 Staffel 2.(H)/14 had to come from the Reich.

Due to a shortage of aircraft, the Luftwaffe employed numbers of captured enemy machines. This ex-French Armée de l'Air Caudron C-445 Goéland was employed as a liaison aircraft.

Rear hatch open, a Go 242 is waiting to be loaded at Eleusis. After a stopover in Crete, this Schleppschwarm Afrika glider would be towed to Africa by a Ju 52.

The German fighter force, comprising at the outset just a single Bf 110 Gruppe, III./ZG 26, I./JG 27, arrived in Africa during April 1941. The launch of *Marita/Merkur* and then *Barbarossa* would complicate things at a time when the Afrika Korps seemed ready to push toward Alexandria. Units belonging to X. Fliegerkorps were indeed posted to the new Eastern Front while the Ju 88 twins of III./KG 30 (which had participated in the bombing of Tobruk) and the nightfighter Bf 110s of I./NJG 3 had also departed the Mediterranean theater to return to the Europe.

As the RAF/SAAF/RAAF gradually strengthened after *Merkur*, I./JG 27, despite its many aces, was still flying the older Emil variants of the Bf 109. II./JG 27 was thus transferred from Russia and in September arrived in Africa with its more modern Bf 109 F "Friedrichs" replacing 7./JG 26 that returned to France. And, to complete the Ju 87 Stuka complement, I./St.G. 3 arrived to support the other two dive-bomber groups. Some interim solutions were also put in place. In September a detachment of I./KG 40 with six Fw 200s was dispatched to the front, which proved a relative failure.

But, in continuously strengthening German aviation in Africa, X. Fliegerkorps (who had transferred from Sicily to Greece/Crete) had neglected the thorn that was Malta. Subject since mid-1941 to the attentions of Regia Aeronautica bombers alone, this "natural aircraft carrier in the Mediterranean" had recovered from the brink and, thanks to the information provided by Ultra, its bombers and torpedo planes were able to seriously disrupt maritime and air traffic resupplying the German African army. Ju 52 transports were being shot down and freighters loaded with matériel and tankers with their cargoes of fuel vital to a war of movement were being sent to the seabed. Serious problems of resupply were appearing, which Rommel seemed not to fully appreciate as he overstretched his lines eastward. However, on October 24, in a letter to the FHQ (Führer's headquarters), General Enno von Rintelen echoed the fears of Mussolini and the Italian Commando Supremo about the growing lack of protection for convoys in the Mediterranean.

At that time, given the difficulties of supplying Africa, a "Schleppschwarm Afrika" had been set up at Hildesheim with half a dozen Go 242 gliders and an equivalent number of Ju 52s from KGzbV 1, a unit based at Eleusis in Athens that operated shuttles between Greece and Derna to bring in reinforcements and supplies to the desert while flying wounded personnel back if necessary. The aircraft stopped over at Heraklion in Crete and, between here and Derna, occasionally had a Bf 110 escort from III./ZG 26. The "Schwarm" was supposed to be supported by Go.Kdo/X. Fliegerkorps also based at Eleusis. But this little "commando" had only two Gothas on strength in total.

Probably taken in Derna, this shot shows a Go 242 glider lost among a group of Ju 88s probably from LG 1.

Strength of opposing air forces on the eve of *Crusader*

Aircraft subordinated to the Fl.F. Afrika, November 15, 1941*

1.(F)/121 (det.) 6 (3)*	
2.(H)/14	? (?)
III./LG 1	19 (2)
Stab St.G. 3	3 (3)
I./St.G. 1	31 (15)
II./St.G. 2	34 (19)
I./St.G. 3	26 (26)
I./JG 27	10 (5)
II./JG 27	25 (22)
III./ZG 26 (1 Staffel)	12 (7)
III./KGzbV 1 (det.)	11 (6)

* Based on Gundelach.

** Figures in brackets indicate serviceable aircraft.

Gundelach has I./St.G. 3 attached to X. Fliegerkorps but documents prove the Gruppe was indeed in Africa during this time frame.

The temporary weakness of I./JG 27 is explained by the absence of pilots who were training on the Bf 109 F. The Gruppe thus depleted comprised a single Staffel.

In case of serious problems, Fl.F. Afrika could count on the support of X. Fl.K. but it was limited to the remainder of LG 1 and the other two Staffeln of III./ZG 26.

2.(F)/123 operated from Greece/Crete.

Strength of Commonwealth fighter units in the desert, mid-November 1941

253 Wing: 208, 237 & 451 Squadrons (Hurricane)

258 Wing: 1 SAAF, 94, 238 & 274 Squadrons (Hurricane)

2 SAAF & 3 RAAF (Tomahawk)

262 Wing: 4 SAAF, 112 & 250 Squadrons (Tomahawk)

80 Squadron (Hurribombers)

229 & 260 Squadrons (Hurricane)

269 Wing: 30 & RN(F) Squadrons (Hurricane & Martlet)

Additional: 33 Squadron (Hurricane) and elements of 272 Squadron (Beaufighter)

General Stefan Fröhlich (second from left), Fliegerführer Afrika, in conversation with Ofw. Richard Heller, one of the aces of 8./ZG 26 and a recipient of the Knight's Cross in August 1941. ZG 26 was to suffer heavy losses during *Crusader*.

During their advance, Allied troops captured large numbers of wrecked German aircraft like this Ju 52 probably destroyed in an air raid.

A Ju 88 C of I./NJG 2 (coded R4) at Derna. In December 1941, these aircraft arrived as reinforcements but were in Africa only for a week.

Operation *Crusader* Opens

On November 18, 1941, *Crusader* opened with powerful attacks on Axis airfields by Maryland and Blenheim bombers escorted by Tomahawks. Many aircraft were destroyed on the ground and, although two bombers were claimed by I./JG 27, the Axis fighter response was muted. Heavy rain had bogged down much of the Luftwaffe and Regia Aeronautica on the forward airfields, and frequent strafing and bombing attacks by Beaufighters and Tomahawks quickly cut the number of aircraft available. Soon, however, some of the heaviest fighting yet seen in the desert broke out, on land and in the air.

Rommel, taken by surprise, initially doubted the reality of this new offensive and did not give adequate orders. It was not until November 20 that resistance stiffened, but Luftwaffe losses were mounting. On that day, between El Adem and Acroma, some 20 P-40s from 112 Squadron RAF and 3 Squadron RAAF fought half a dozen 8./ZG 26 Bf 110 Es. Four *Zerstörer* were shot down (two radio operators were wounded). One Tomahawk crashed on returning to base and while another was seriously damaged.

In the days that followed, British ground forces pushed toward Tobruk to break the siege.

Having grasped the danger, the German high command sent what it could. Thus, on November 21, six Ju 88 nightfighters from 2./NJG 2 deployed to Berca (Benghazi) under command of Hptm. Harmstorf. These twin-engined nightfighters had just arrived from the Netherlands, flying into Catania, Sicily, to operate over Malta. However, in recognition of the urgency of the need to collect information on the enemy advance, they were re-routed to Libya. But, due to maintenance difficulties, these Ju 88s returned to Sicily a mere week later.

On November 21, enemy pressure was such that the Ju 88s of I. and II./LG 1 left Greece to transfer to Benina to support III./LG 1 already present on African soil. On November 22, the German fighters regrouped. I. and II./JG 27 claimed no less than 14 P-40s and seven Blenheims that day. Other enemy losses included four Blenheims, one Wellington, five Hurricanes and a dozen Tomahawks as well as two Blenheims destroyed on the ground as a result of the combined actions of fighters, including Italian, and antiaircraft fire. JG 27 lost six aircraft (two captured, one killed, and one wounded).

On November 23, II./JG 27 suffered a grievous loss when Kommandeur Hptm. Wolfgang Lippert was shot down near Bir el Gubi. Seriously wounded, he died in a British hospital on December 3, 1941. On November 24, Ofw. Richard Heller, one of

Hptm. Wolfgang Lippert (seen here at Karinhall, residence of Hermann Göring, for the presentation of his Knight's Cross) was shot down and captured on November 23, 1941. The Kommandeur of II./ JG 27 succumbed to his injuries in a British hospital.

III./JG 27 in turn arrived in Africa to join forces with the other two Gruppen of the Geschwader. From left: Hptm. Erhard Braune (Kommandeur III./JG 27), Oblt. Gustav Rödel (Kapitän 4./JG 27), Hptm. Edu Neumann (Kommandeur I./JG 27) and Oblt. Gerhard Homuth (Kapitän 3./JG 27).

8./ZG 26's best pilots, had to crash-land his Bf 110 in the desert. He was wounded but was recovered with his radio operator by ground troops and returned to combat.

Luftwaffe's losses continued to mount until the end of the month, due not only to aerial combat but also to continuous raids against the airfields—such as that of Derna on August 28—and antiaircraft fire. The Bf 110s of III./ZG 26 were committed wholesale and, having to fly at low altitude to machine-gun enemy columns and positions, were vulnerable to ground fire. On November 26, I. and II./LG 1 were scheduled to return to Eleusis. The next day, Rommel was indeed forced to withdraw his troops to the Tobruk line and, given this withdrawal, it seemed wiser to repatriate these two Gruppen back to Europe. This did not prevent the Ju 88s from continuing to carry out missions against British positions to slow the enemy advance. The lack of fuel and ammunition was becoming a key difficulty for the Afrika Korps.

Hasty Reinforcement

On October 31, Hitler sent a message to Mussolini announcing the appointment of Feldmarschall Albert Kesselring as head of the Luftflottekommando 2 (HQ Messina) and the deployment of Luftflotte 2 under General der Flieger Bruno Loerzer to the Mediterranean, in an attempt to limit the severe losses on the supply routes to Africa. This air force based in Sicily was to be dedicated solely to neutralizing the island of Malta. But even then, the Luftwaffe—which was largely involved in the USSR—could barely expand in the Mediterranean theater and the constitution of II. Fl.K. took several weeks. This did not help Rommel, who demanded urgent reinforcements. Hence the temporary and urgent dispatch to Africa of 2./NJG 2.

A Bf 109 F of III./JG 53 seen overflying the Alps en route to Africa via Sicily.

Although up against opponents far superior in numbers, the Hs 126 of 2.(H)/14 continued their difficult but essential missions, several being lost. In late 1941, they were supplanted by Bf 110s.

On December 2, the Führer promulgated *Kriegsweisung* (War Directive) No. 38 ordering the reinforcement of German Axis air assets in the Mediterranean. This was easier said than done. On December 3, Feldmarschall Kesselring came to review the units present in Sicily, hoping to engage his aircraft over Malta as soon as possible. There was some urgency since, in November, 63 percent of cargo destined for Libya had been sent to the bottom of the sea. This was at a time when the Axis in Africa was under pressure from the enemy and being gradually forced backward.

Also on December 2, III./JG 53, led by Hptm. Wolf-Dietrich Wilcke, previously based in the Netherlands, arrived at Catania, via Munich and Treviso. The airmen of the "Pik As" (Ace of Spades) were welcomed with open arms in Sicily. But III./JG 53 had not flown in to fight over Malta but were in transit, assigned to support the Afrika Korps as a matter of priority.

Fighting continued in the skies over North Africa. On December 4, III./ZG 26 lost Kommandeur Maj. Karl Kaschka, who was killed along with his radio operator. Kaschka was already leading the Gruppe when it was transferred to the Mediterranean. On December 6, III./JG 27 under Hptm. Erhard Braune arrived at Tmimi, having been detached from the Eastern Front. All three Gruppen of JG 27 were now in the African theater.

On December 8, III./JG 53 arrived at Tmimi via Heraklion. The North African campaign got off to a bad start for the "Pik As" as two Ju 52s carrying the unit's ground staff were shot down along with their passengers. The Gruppe was forced to rely mainly

Lt Hermann Weber of 9./ZG 26. His Bf 110 crashed at Derna on December 8.

In Profile:
Fighter aircraft

Bf 109E-7/Trop of I./JG27 flown by
Oblt Ludwig Franzisket.

Bf 109E-7/B/Trop of 7./ZG 1.

Bf 109F-4/Trop of II./JG 27.

Fw 200 Condors of I./KG 40 returned to Africa in December 1941 not as bombers but as fuel carriers.

on mechanics from JG 27 who were already overwhelmed with the maintenance of their own aircraft. Only one mission could be carried out on departure from Tmimi before the emergency evacuation of this airfield ahead of the advance of British troops. However, among other things, four Bf 109 Friedrichs of III./JG 53 had to be scuttled to prevent them falling intact into enemy hands. They were not the only ones.

But the strengthening of the fighter force was not the most important priority: ensuring essential supplies was. Unable to act quickly and effectively against Malta, the tempo of air transport arrangements had to be upped. According to F. Morzik, "resupply by sea was handicapped by the action of British aircraft and submarines … It was impossible to move units from other fronts so new transport units were established as a matter of urgency, utilizing training or anti-shipping machines." In Munich-Riem, KGzbV 400 and 500 were created and immediately dispatched to Foggia, Brindisi, and Trapani. Thus, six I./KG 40 aircraft left France once again, not to operate as bombers but as transport aircraft. Their role was very effective as confirmed by a British report in early 1942: "A prisoner reports that the movement of Rommel's army in January 1942 was probably made possible by the shuttle flights operated by Fw 200s from Catania to the Arco Philaenorum to transport fuel. Five aircraft operated three shuttles of this type per day, on each occasion flying in 15,000 liters of petrol."

The He 111s of II./KG 26 based in Greece had, over the previous weeks, continued their attacks on Egypt, the Suez Canal, and Tobruk. In December, they were deployed as fuel transporters to the Afrika Korps, carrying containers under their wings or in their fuselages. However, the Löwengeschwader's aircraft could not be fully engaged because, like the Ju

The He 111s of II./KG 26 were also employed for the transport of fuel supplies.

Aircrew losses were high on both sides. This is a Luftwaffe cemetery, probably near Derna.

A Go 242 captured in the desert. British army experts were able to examine this transport glider for the first time, leading to enhancements in the equivalent RAF machines.

A Bf 110 of III./ZG 26 captured apparently intact at its aerodrome. A RAF nightfighter unit was to test one of the captured *Zerstörer*, noting that it was faster than the Beaufighter at altitude but slower at ground level.

This Ju 87 of 3./St.G. 1, with the "diving raven" emblem, found at Acroma also seems not to have been scuttled. During *Crusader*, the British estimated that more than 500 Axis aircraft were captured, most of these in the form of wrecks on airfields.

88s of LG 1, they had to perform other equally important tasks such as convoy protection, maritime strikes and reconnaissance and attacks (often at night) against British positions in North Africa.

Increasing transport capacity was vital but losses were high following the interventions of the RAF based on Malta, well informed as it was by Ultra. On September 12 alone, four Ju 52s were shot down. More often than not transporter crews perished with their machines. The few gliders of the "Schleppschwarm Afrika" henceforth operated from Italy and no longer from Eleusis. However, during one enemy push, the crews were forced to hurriedly embark in Ju 52s to return to Europe as quickly as possible, abandoning their Go 242 gliders. About ten of these machines fell more or less intact into enemy hands, enabling the British to examine the Gotha 242 for the first time. Having lost all its gliders, "Schleppschwarm Afrika" was then disbanded.

The Bf 109 Friedrichs of JG 27 and III/JG 53 flew large numbers of sorties and pilots' kill totals grew accordingly—the kill claims filed regularly list the names of aces such as Marseille, Wilcke, Neuhoff, and Espenlaub. However, this was not enough to stop the Afrika Korps from retreating. At that time, the first Tomahawks were engaged in Libya. But while they were fast at lower altitudes and packed a heavier punch than any RAF fighters in theater, except the Beaufighter, they soon proved to be no match for a well-flown Bf 109 F.

German bombers were in constant action. On December 11, Ju 88s of I./LG 1 were airborne from Eleusis for Tmimi. After refueling, four bombers attacked a concentration of armor near Bir Hakeim and, having dropped their loads, vehicles were machine-gunned and strafed. However, six Tomahawks from 250 Squadron and the Hurricanes of the Royal Navy

Ofw. Albert Espenlaub was one of the aces of 1./JG 27, credited with 14 kills over North Africa.

Espenlaub had to land his Bf 109 F "white 11" near El Adem and was captured. He was shot dead while attempting to escape.

Ju 88 A-4 L1+HK of 2./LG 1 seen during a transfer flight to Derna.

Following the death in action of Kommandeur Kaschka and the unexplained disappearance of his successor Steinberger three weeks later, Hptm. Georg Christl (right) was appointed to take command of III./ZG 26.

Erbo Graf von Kageneck (9./JG 27) photographed here in May 1941 while flying operations over Malta from Sicily. Note his kill tally on the rudder of his Emil. During the fighting in North Africa, JG 27 would fly the latest variant of the Bf 109 series, specifically the "F" or "Friedrich."

fighter squadrons were soon on the scene. A Ju 88 was shot down and the crew captured. Tmimi was soon after machine-gunned by fighters, a Ju 88 being destroyed on the ground. Following their raid, the Ju 88s landed in Derna. For its part, II./LG 1, with a good fighter escort, bombed vehicle columns near Tobruk. That evening, most of the Ju 88 LG 1s in Africa returned to Eleusis, a safe distance from the front.

On December 12, fighting raged in the air, both in support of the British advance and to ease the pressure on the Axis lines. 7. and 9. Staffeln of JG 53 claimed no fewer than six Hurricanes and one Curtiss P-40. It is likely that the Bf 109s were in fact confronted with only Tomahawks from 112 Squadron RAF and 3 Squadron RAAF which lost five machines during the afternoon. In the chaos of dogfighting, identification had become difficult for pilots who had not had the time to adapt to this type of war.

On December 13 came another blow for I./JG 27 which lost Ofw. Albert Espenlaub, a veteran with 14 kills. He was forced to put down his Friedrich near El Adem and was taken captive. The ferocity of the fighting was such that fatigue and bitterness led to a number of incidents: on December 14, Ofw. Hermann Förster, one of the first airmen of 2./JG 27 to arrive in Africa and an ace with 13 kills, was shot and killed as he parachuted down after combat near Tmimi. During the Phoney War, Förster had been a pilot with 11(N)./JG 2, an experimental nightfighter unit where he was credited with five kills. On the night of December 15/16, the Allied advance was such that the remnants of III./LG 1 still present in Benina were ordered to fly to Eleusis. The following night, mining of Tobruk's harbor was carried out. Despite concentrated antiaircraft fire, no Ju 88s were hit.

On December 16, Allied antiaircraft fire brought down the Kapitän of 7./JG 53, Oblt. Heinz Altendorf. This ace with 14 kills belly-landed his machine near El Mechili before being captured.

Since it was self-evident that the Luftwaffe fighters could not stop the enemy's advance and that III./JG 53 was sustaining heavy losses with no results, the Gruppe began its return to Catania to support the rest of the "Pik As" which had begun operations against Malta. On December 17, the RAF, RAAF, and SAAF launched a massive, continuous three-day attack on the retreating Axis troops.

In Gambut, the British "liberated" this Hurricane, V7670, reported lost in July 1941. It seems hardly to have been used by its temporary owners, nor has a swastika been painted on the tailfin.

Crusader Runs Out of Steam

Despite the losses of men and equipment, heavy RAF bombing raids and airfield attacks by the Long Range Desert Group (LRDG) and the SAS, the Axis air forces did not collapse, even after the withdrawal of III./JG 53 and LG 1. However, the RAF and Commonwealth air forces continued to strengthen. For example, on December 27, 3 Squadron RAAF reached Msus with brand-new Kittyhawks.

On December 24, the Luftwaffe lost two important officers. The Kommandeur of III./ZG 26, Hptm. Thomas Steinberger, had taken off that day from Tatoi, probably returning from taking his instructions from X. Fliegerkorps HQ at Athens-Kyfissia. En route to Crete, the twin-engined machine disappeared with its three occupants without trace, probably the victim of a technical problem. III./ZG 26 was then taken over at short notice by Hptm. Georg Christl. The other critical loss was Kapitän of 9./JG 27, Oblt. Erbo Graf von Kageneck, who was seriously wounded in combat but managed to land his aircraft. Immediately transferred to a hospital in Naples, he died of blood poisoning on January 12, 1942.

At the end of the year, both sides were in need of rest and refit. While RAF bombers units were urgently summoned to the Far East, in view of the developing Japanese military situation, III./LG 1, heavily depleted by the fighting, flew into Salonika-Sedes to rest. The aircraft were transferred to a brand-new IV./LG 1 before its personnel were sent back for *Auffrischung* (refit) in the Reich. Fighting continued into early 1942 but *Crusader* had more or less officially petered out by January 8.

Realizing that the British were about to launch a new attack on his forces at Agedabia, Rommel forestalled them by pulling his troops back to strong positions at El Agheila, on January 6, 1942.

British lines of communication were extended to the limit, and with reinforcements and supplies curtailed dramatically due to the entry of Japan into the war, their advance necessarily stalled. They were now were in much the same position as they had been in February 1941, and in a similar dangerously weakened state.

An image that sums up *Crusader*: a Marmon Herrington self-propelled carrier tractor passes the wreck of one of the many Ju 87s lost at the end of 1941.

Lt. Werner Schroer (1./JG 27) seen inspecting an Fi 156 of the Wüstennotstaffel, a dedicated desert search and rescue unit.

Assessment of *Crusader*

For many historians Operation *Crusader* was but one episode of this desert war which, between 1941 and 1943, alternated between rapid advances and sudden retreats. However, *Crusader* was a bad omen for the Wehrmacht, heralding the scheduled end of the German adventure in Africa. As Shores points out, extending its lines in the desert was only conceivable if sufficient and continuous reinforcements and supplies were available. In February 1941, the British army had no reserves. During *Crusader*, Auchinleck legitimately believed he had, but that he was "betrayed" by Pearl Harbor and the Japanese assault on British positions in the Far East.

Rommel, on the other hand, neglected the problem of supply far too much and, worse, attracted Luftwaffe units to Africa that would have been more useful in Sicily operating against Malta or the USSR. The North African front now took on such a dimension that the three Gruppen of JG 53 as well as II. and III./JG 27 departed Russia in support of the Afrika Korps, further weakening the Eastern Front. The aerial battles of *Crusader* had been bloody for both sides, and depleted both, but exceptional German fighter aces such as Lippert, Espenlaub, Förster, Altendorf, and von Kageneck had been lost. Such Kommandeure, Kapitäne and experienced veterans were very difficult to replace.

A special mission

I./LG 1 was not only deployed to bomb British lines in Libya. On January 21, a special mission was ordered for the crews. According to Ofw. Heinz Garich:

> On the evening of January 20, we were summoned to a meeting at HQ in Eleusis. I. Gruppe was entrusted with a special mission. According to informants, the British HQ was located in a very pleasant villa near Barce. In the early morning, I./LG 1 was supposed to take off to destroy it. We had 12 aircraft and took to the air at 4 a.m. with four bombs weighing 250 kilos. This covert mission imposed radio silence. But, while taxiing out for takeoff, the machine ahead of us got its gear stuck in a stretch of sandy ground and came to a standstill. I had to do the same. It took time to move the aircraft and I took off half an hour later than the rest of the formation. I reached the African coast at low altitude but the wind had blown me 40 kilometers farther east. Through gaps in the clouds, I could nevertheless spot the road leading to the HQ. I found the area intact and was surprised that my comrades had not already attacked. I overflew the target and dropped two bombs. There was antiaircraft fire but I made a second pass to dump the last two. I could not take pictures of the attack because my machine gunner was not one of my regular crew and he had no camera. I returned to Eleusis—by this time of course nobody was waiting for me. I learned then that, given the clouds and bad weather, the operation had been a failure, as no one had been able to locate the target. Oblt. Iro Ilk was therefore stunned when I made my report. He had already reported the lack of success to the Fliegerkorps and contacted the air corps commander again to inform him of my attack. Shortly afterward, a staff officer came to visit us and awarded my crew and myself an Iron Cross First Class (EK I) that we received on February 26.

In Profile: Bombers

He 111 H-6 of 6./KG 26.

Ju 87 R-2 of 4./St.G. 2.

Ju 88A-4 of 1./LG 1.

A group of paratroopers from the Kampfgruppe Burckhardt shortly before boarding a Ju 52 to Africa.

As *Crusader* ended, the Wehrmacht was still stuck fast in front of Moscow by "General Winter." Maintaining forces in numbers on these two fronts was a challenge. The Wehrmacht could only hope that the planned 1942 spring offensive toward the Caucasus would shake up the Red Army in whole or in part, thus allowing German units on the Eastern Front to be withdrawn and sent to Africa.

The Fallschirmjäger, lacking heavy equipment, had to be supported with equipment, such as this Italian army truck, which here has bogged down and had to be towed by an NSU tracked motorcycle.

But if the Japanese had entered the war in December 1941, the same was true of the United States, who, under the guise of Lend-Lease, had supported the British war effort from the beginning of the conflict. Now that the United States had officially entered the war, its industrial-scale military production was set to ramp up—for the greater benefit of its allies in London and Moscow.

The Odyssey of Kampfgruppe Burckhardt

One of the consequences of *Crusader* was the deployment of paratroopers to Africa. Since the blood-letting of Crete in May 1941, the Fallschirmjäger were no longer brought into battle by air but fought as elite infantrymen. In December, while II./Fliegerkorps was being urgently set up in Sicily, an antitank detachment of the Fallschirm-Lehr-Batallion was assembled and placed under the command of Maj. Walter Burckhardt. This "Kampfgruppe Burckhardt" was issued tropical equipment, the men were vaccinated and, via Italy, arrived aboard Ju 52s at Castel Benito on January 7, a day before the end of *Crusader*. By truck, this detachment reached the front and fought sporadically until mid-March. The battle group returned to Germany via Derna on March 21.

This improvised dispatch of Fallschirm-jäger to North Africa was not a success. Many parachutists fell victim to tropical diseases such as diarrhoea and

A moment of rest for Kampfgruppe Burckhardt. Note the Panzerjäger unit's small recoilless antitank gun.

A Bf 109 F of I./JG 27 is examined by Italian soldiers.

On January 16, Hptm. Joachim Helbig, commander of I./LG 1, received the Oak Leaves. This leader was as much appreciated by his men as he was feared by the Allies who apparently dubbed Lehrgeschwader I "Helbig's flyers."

malaria, and had difficulty acclimatizing to desert conditions. Their equipment proved unsuitable and their unbalanced diet caused various disorders, including scurvy. Nevertheless, this deployment enabled some preparation for paratroop deployments in late 1942/early 1943 in Tunisia.

Another Lull

Taking advantage of the relative calm, the Luftwaffe reorganized and attempted to fill the gaps in its ranks. Refurbishment and reinforcement and standardization weree carried out. I./St.G. 1 became II./St.G. 3 while II./St.G. 2 was redesignated III./St.G. 3. Having evacuated to better-equipped aerodromes, JG 27 regrouped and again showed its teeth. On January 9, three Kittyhawks and four Hurricanes were downed without loss.

Despite the sandstorms that developed during this period, the Bf 109s persisted. On January 14, eight Hurricanes (including seven from 94 Squadron alone) were shot down—still without loss to the *Tagjagd*. On January 16, the repeated actions of I./LG 1 were recognized at the highest level when Kommander Helbig was awarded the Oak Leaves to the Knight's Cross. On the same day, the Ju 88s left Eleusis for Heraklion before returning to Libya to bomb columns near El Daba. However, two Ju 88s were shot down by fighters.

However, despite its remarkable fighting spirit, the Luftwaffe's fighter arm remained weak. On January 16, the Stab (Staff, or headquarters unit) and the three Gruppen of JG 27 had a theoretical strength of some 70 Bf 109 Friedrichs—only 18 of which were serviceable. The Geschwader was supported by five Bf 109s from the Jabostaffel/JG 53 (four aircraft serviceable). III./ZG 26 could only muster eight Bf 110s (four serviceable). During January, there was only one *Zerstörer* Staffel left in Africa, the other two having returned to Sicily to operate over Malta. From that point on, the few available aircraft were placed to a large extent in the hands of the "aces" who were able to counter superior numbers of Allied aircraft thanks largely to their own skills and experience.

Ju 88 LG 1 crew seen prior to a sortie from Eleusis.

With Rommel back on the offensive, battlefield tactical reconnaissance assumed a key role. Here a camera is being loaded into a Bf 110 from 2.(H)/14.

Rommel on the Offensive

With the British offensive over, Rommel now sought to take advantage of the arrival of a supply convoy at Tripoli on January 5, 1942 to return to the offensive. In this, he opposed Feldmarschall Kesselring's wishes to give priority to neutralizing or even capturing Malta. Cairo or Malta? This was to be the bone of contention in the Axis high command in the Mediterranean. So with no orders, with more or less reconstituted units and a very random supply operation, the "Desert Fox" launched his forces westward and entered Benghazi on January 29, thus taking over control from the British. To enable this, anything in the Mediterranean theater that could fly was assigned to North Africa. On January 27, 12./LG 1, which appears to have been very active at that time, left Eleusis for the Libyan field aerodrome at Merd.

On January 30, 12./LG 1 flew into Arco and, from there, attacked British columns on the coastal road near Derna and, above all, on the famous "Serpentine," the winding road leading to the plateau. To compensate for the lack of bombers, in addition to the few "Jabo" dive-bombers of JG 53, Bf 109s of JG 27 were also deployed as fighter-bombers.

2.(H)/14 received a number of Bf 109 Emils on an "experimental" basis.

Due to the lack of single-engined fighters, the *Zerstörer*, often operating as Jabos, were regularly escorted by Regia Aeronautica aircraft (here a Fiat G.50).

Bombs are hung on the belly of a Bf 110 of III./ZG 26 operating in the Jabo role. In the desert, everything was done by hand under very primitive conditions.

Early February saw Axis attacks on Gazala and Mersa Matruh. Finally, on February 3, the British evacuated Mashili. In the weeks that followed, various deployments took place on the ground, but with neither side having enough troops in an offensive position, a precarious balance was established. On February 7, I./JG 27 deployed to Martuba and, from this airfield, the young ace Körner shot down a Blenheim near Derna. On February 10, while Cyrenaica had been almost entirely recaptured by the Afrika Korps, 7./ZG 26 lost another veteran when the machine flown by its Kapitän, Oblt. Ludwig Schotte, exploded in mid-air, probably following the premature arming of his bomb. The *Zerstörer* were operating as Jabos because of the lack of bombers proper.

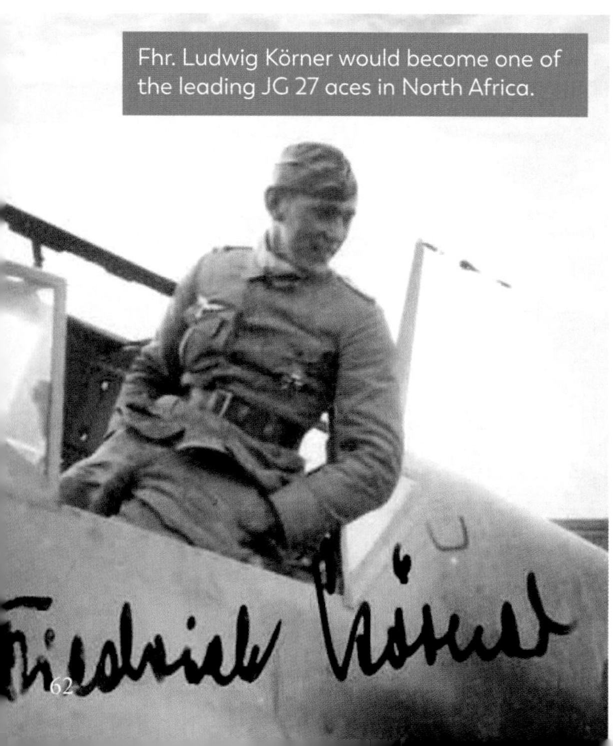

Fhr. Ludwig Körner would become one of the leading JG 27 aces in North Africa.

Operations from Greece (LG 1 and 2.(F)/123) continued, often at night, over Egypt. But the RAF had received radar-equipped Beaufighters and losses of German intruders would increase.

As the British army had to ensure its supplies, LG 1 stepped up its attacks against maritime traffic. Thus, on February 13, 12./LG 1 participated in an attack against ships anchored in Tobruk harbor,

On February 22, the so-called "Star of Africa," Hans-Joachim Marseille, was awarded the Knight's Cross.

being countered by Hurricanes of 73 Squadron. On the same day, a series of attacks was launched against a convoy leaving Alexandria.

On February 22, having returned 50 kills, Lt. Hans-Joachim Marseille was finally awarded the Knight's Cross. He then enjoyed a spell of leave in Germany and attended senior officer training courses, which kept him away from the North African front for several weeks. His comrades, however, continued to see the lion's share of combat in the skies over Libya.

Although aerial clashes were sporadic, the RAF responded to the night attacks against Alexandria or Suez by pounding—also at night—German aerodromes. Several Wellingtons were lost (as on February 24 and 25) to the ever-present Flak defenses. On February 28, I./LG 1 attacked various targets in the Sidi Barrani sector. A lone Ju 88 on a coastal reconnaissance had the misfortune to clash with 805 Squadron Martlets and was reported missing, along with its crew.

In early March, I./LG 1 was split between Sicily (to attack Malta) and Heraklion (to attack Africa and the convoys between Alexandria, Malta and Gibraltar). The "Helbig flyers" would soon prove to be one of the most formidable and feared opponents of the Royal Navy. The Libyan Sea—between Crete and the African coast—came to be dubbed "Bomb Alley" by Royal Navy sailors and cargo crews in the convoys that suffered incessant bombing attacks.

A twin-engined Wellington shot down by the Flak. Antiaircraft guns were essential in protecting aerodromes regularly attacked at night by RAF bombers: the Luftwaffe deployed no aircraft in the night-fighting role in North Africa.

The temporary departure of Lt. Marseille did not end the supremacy of I./JG 27. Thus, on March 13, while five Hurricanes and 12 Kittyhawks were flying cover over Tobruk, two Bf 109s dove from the clouds. Ofw. Otto Schulz claimed one Allied fighter downed. To counter these dangerous fighters, the British army responded with nighttime bombardments but also deployed commandos against Axis airfields.

March 7, 1942 is a key date in the history of the defense of Malta and the war in the Mediterranean. On this day, the aircraft carrier HMS *Eagle* launched Spitfires to strengthen the island's defenses, in Operation *Spotter*, the first fighters of this type to reinforce the RAF in this theater. The British high command understood the importance of Malta, which was crucially disrupting supplies destined for the Afrika Korps. The Luftwaffe therefore had to redouble its efforts to subdue the island but it was becoming increasingly apparent that it could not effectively cover two tasks: fighting in North Africa and over Malta.

March had been relatively calm, enabling the opposing air forces to rebuild and regroup after the serious losses incurred during Operation *Crusader*. April saw a stiffening of the fighting. On April 2, JG 27 flew no fewer than 99 sorties that included mounting drop tanks to fly convoy-protection sorties, free hunts, strafing, and bomber escorts. On April 18, I./JG 27 "celebrated" its first year in the desert.

By early April, 2.(H)/14, which had also arrived a year earlier in Africa, was exhausted and returned to Europe; its last loss in Africa at that time was on March 21. In Vienna-Schwechat, it was reorganized and gave up its Bf 110s, converting to the Bf 109 Gustav. The Staffel also transferred some personnel to its replacement, 4.(H)/12, mainly observers who were surplus to requirements given that the unit was now flying single-seaters. Equipped with the Bf 110/Bf 109, 4.(H)/12 arrived from Russia and was immediately thrown into combat. The Staffel quickly discovered the realities of war in this new theater as, as early as April 20, one of the unit's Bf 109 E-7s was shot down over Naduret el Ghascenase by a Hurricane of 80 Squadron. On April 23, a Bf 110 E-3 was lost near Bir el Chanalat in a sandstorm (crew killed) and the next day, a second Bf 109 pilot was shot down and killed near Gazala by Tomahawks.

A Bf 109 of II./JG 3 in Sicily. 6./JG 3 would support JG 27 for nearly three weeks, unsuccessfully.

In April, II./KG 100 departed France for Greece. From Kalamaki, its He 111s flew sorties over North Africa using Libyan bases as stopovers.

On April 7, Bf 109s from 6./JG 3 landed at Martuba. II./JG 3 was then operating from Sicily over Malta; this Gruppe was diverted to Africa in support of JG 27. Its aircraft would fly free hunts and escorts but also flew Jabo missions. 6./JG 3 lost two pilots in Africa (including one taken captive) and appeared not to have been able to act with any effectiveness. The unit returned to Sicily on April 26.

On April 13, 7./ZG 26 committed six of its aircraft—probably all that the Staffel could get airworthy—for a special mission. In order to counter an LRDG infiltration in the Libyan desert, the twin-engined aircraft were to escort two Savoia Marchetti SM.82 from 145th Gruppo carrying some 60 Italian-German combat engineers. The two transports touched down on an abandoned airfield with three of the Bf 110s while the other three orbited the area as top cover. The pioneers destroyed various fuel and ammunition dumps before returning home without difficulty.

During the months of March and April, Lehrgeschwader 1 had to split its aircraft between attacks on Africa and Malta. While its Ju 88s escalated their offensive actions, it was not enough. By early April 1942, the He 111s of II./KG 100 had joined the Stab/ KG 100 in France (Chartres) and this unit, ready for combat, would soon be committed to raids against the United Kingdom or else sent to join forces with I./KG 100 in Russia (Saki). However, the military situation was such that the new unit was suddenly split, II./

A JG 27 Bf 109 kicks up clouds of sand as it gets airborne.

Oblt. Rudolf Braun, one of the oldest Stuka aces, was awarded the Knight's Cross on June 14, 1941. He was leading 1./St.G. 3 when he was seriously wounded on April 25, 1942 over Tobruk, being forced to leave the desert theater. After leading various units, he survived the war.

KG 100 being sent to the Mediterranean while the Stab/KG 100 was dispatched to reinforce I. Gruppe in the USSR. The Luftwaffe now had to constantly juggle the units at its disposal like pieces on a chessboard, occasionally shifting them in a sometimes apparently arbitrary manner. On April 21, 26 He 111 H-6 bombers of II./KG 100 flew into the Athenian airfield at Kalamaki. Contacts were quickly made and equipment prepared for sorties as rapidly as possible. On April 24, the first attack was launched from Greece against Quoteifya in Libya with a stopover in Crete for refueling. The tone was set from the start. During this raid, a Heinkel came down into the sea with its crew. On the night of April 28/29, II./KG 100 bombed Alexandria with the support of Ju 88s of I./LG 1. 89 Squadron shot down a Ju 88 and an He 111. Egypt's night defenses had been greatly strengthened to counter raids emanating mainly from Greece and Crete. And the use of radar and information from Ultra made operations in this sector a risky entreprise for the Luftwaffe.

The Luftwaffe also reinforced its night protection. As raids by Wellingtons became more and more of an issue, the Ju 88 nightfighters of 2./NJG 2 departed Sicily to base up at Derna.

On April 25, heavy clashes occurred between RAF and Luftwaffe fighters, the latter flying top cover for the Ju 87 Stukas of St. G. 3 raiding Tobruk. Lt. Jochen Marseille, back from leave, returned several more kills. Nevertheless, no fewer than six severely damaged Ju 87s had to make crash-landings. Critically wounded Knight's Cross recipient Rudolf Braun was able to bring his aircraft back to base, with his radio operator dead, but subsequently had to be repatriated as a result of his injuries.

The beginning of May saw continuous Luftwaffe attacks against Egypt. On the night of May 1/2, Port Said was raided by Ju 88s of LG 1 with He 111 bombers of II./KG 26. A Ju 88 fell victim to a Beaufighter of 203 Squadron. On May 2, I./LG 1 conducted various operations from Crete, attacking the railway stations at Fort Capuzzo and Mersa Matruh, and maritime reconnaissance. On the night of May 3/4, LG 1 and II./KG 100 returned to Alexandria, an He 111 of 5./KG 100 being shot down by antiaircraft fire. The raids continued day and night and, on the night of May 7/8, an LG 1 Ju 88 was lost over Fort Capuzzo, also a victim of antiaircraft fire. Ju 88s of 2. (F) / 123, flying reconnaissance over Egypt, also suffered losses.

A Bf 110 escorting Ju 52 transports. This protection was too often pared back and the transports would suffer as a result.

At this time, the Luftwaffe in the desert comprised:

I./JG 27 x 30 Bf 109 (Martuba)

II./JG 27 x 33 Bf 109 (Martuba)

III./JG 27 x 29 Bf 109 (Martuba)

Jabostaffel x 8 Bf 109 (Martuba)

2./NJG 2 x 9 Ju 88 (Derna)

7./ZG 26 x 12 Bf 110 (Derna)

12./LG 1 x 11 Ju 88 (Berca)

In addition to these Libyan-based units, the Fliegerführer Afrika was able to count on the occasional support of the Crete-based 9./ZG 26 as well as 1. (F) / 121, 2. (F) / 123, LG 1, and II./KG 100. But these units were simultaneously operating over Malta and could not always divert aircraft for African duties. The He 111 torpedo bombers of KG 26 were primarily responsible for attacking convoys. Also at that time, part of the Gruppe was transferred to the Black Sea to harass Soviet shipping. In addition to these resources, Staffeln of Ju 52 flew shuttles between Europe and Africa.

On the opposing side, the RAF had likewise broadened its scope. The North African front, which should have remained secondary, was now becoming increasingly important, as a result of growing enemy activity and heavy air traffic between Italy and Libya. Using information from Ultra decrypts, Beaufighters and Kittyhawks equipped with auxiliary tanks were able to intercept Ju 52 formations at sea, as was the case on May 12, when 15 three-engined transports were claimed. In fact, the formation of KGzbV 1 Ju 52s numbered 14 machines, and was intercepted approaching the African coast with only a weak escort of two Bf 110s. Each trimotor carried 20 passengers. Nine of them were shot down, two more crashed on the coast. The machine piloted by Fw. Günther Frenzel landed near the Lazarett field hospital at Derna where he was immediately treated, four fingers of one hand having been shot away. On December 23, 1942, Frenzel was awarded the Knight's Cross in his hospital bed. An aircraft of 7. / ZG 26 was also shot down in this engagement.

Although he had sustained serious injuries, Fw. Günther Frenzel, a KGzbV 1 pilot, was able to save his Ju 52 with his passengers on May 12, 1942, for which he was awarded the Knight's Cross.

Around May 20, III./JG 53 which operated over Malta from Sicily, was informed of an imminent transfer to Martuba to support JG 27. On May 24, III./ZG 26 had assembled in full at Derna to operate with St.G. 3 and 12./LG 1 in a temporary formation named "Gefechtsverband Sigel" (after the Kommodore of St.G. 3). The following days saw an increase in air activity, heralding the launch of an offensive.

The DAK Attacks the Gazala Line

May 26, 1942, "*Es rommelt wieder!*" ... "Rommel's on the march again!" The Afrika Korps launched a major new offensive to the east. Bir Hakeim and other strongpoints had to be reduced. Every possible aerial asset that could be scraped together, by each side, was thrown into the battle and some of the heaviest air combat yet seen over the desert occured over the course of the following weeks. It was now the turn of Allied fighters to strafe Axis columns on the ground, losing in turn many aircraft: between May 29 and 31, 39 Allied fighters were brought down in this way.

Units based in Greece were involved in the fighting and, on May 27, over Fuka, an He 111 of II./KG 100 fell victim to antiaircraft fire. However, its pilot was able to land and three of the crew were taken captive. Attacks on Sollum, Tobruk, and El Daba followed. In early June 1942, the Heinkels of II./KG 100 were called on to bomb a series of RAF airfields in the desert. To do this, they had to make stopovers in Crete to refuel and rearm.

Newly arrived in Africa, III./JG 53,was deployed on strafing sorties against British positions at Ain el Gazala. Kills were claimed while the pilots of the three Gruppen of JG 27 continued to rack up their *Abschüsse*, their kills.

With the offensive in full swing, the airmen were on edge. In one instance a Ju 88 machine gunner opened up on Oblt. Wilfried Pufahl's machine—designated to fly as escort cover for the same Ju 88. The Kapitän of 7./JG 53 was forced to put down in the desert before being recovered by an Fi 156 of the Wüstennotstaffel.

On May 30, Lt. Jürgen Harder of the "Pik As" wrote in his diary: "We fly four missions from 4:00 to 20:00. We are constantly soaked in sweat. Just sand and sorties. We have no appetite at all due to the heat. But this is Africa and the fighting is tremendous. Armored vehicles, vehicles, infantry, aircraft—just one huge operation. Rommel's plan seems to be going well."

At the beginning of June, III./JG 53 was operating mainly in the Bir Hakeim area defended by French Foreign Legion troops. The Bf 109s furnished escorts for the Ju 87s and 88s bludgeoning the fort and its surroundings, a strongpoint hampering the DAK offensive.

June 1 was a black day for III./ZG 26. The

An Fi 156 of the Wüstennotstaffel flies in to pick up a Bf 109 pilot who has force-landed in the desert.

Oblt. Alfred Wehmeyer, Staka of 7./ZG 26, was killed on June 1, 1942. He was posthumously awarded the Knight's Cross. (via the Wehmeyer family)

On the night of June 8/9, the Kapitän of 4./KG 100, Oblt. Karl Heschl, departed Heraklion to bomb Quoteifya airfield but was forced to ditch his He 111 in the sea off Ras el Keanyig, following engine trouble. The crew was rescued by the British and brought ashore.

Heschl's crew unusually comprised five men, the He 111 carrying a second observer, an officer probably seeking to gain experience ... or promotion.

Oblt. Otto Schulz (4./JG 27), victor in some 50 aerial battles, was reported missing on June 17, 1942 over the desert.

Bf 110s of the Gruppe all appear to have been involved in risky strafing that day, resulting in the loss of three crews. One of the pilots was the talented Oblt. Alfred Wehmeyer, Staka 7./ZG 26. According to the official version, he was caught up in the explosion of an armored vehicle he had just attacked near Martuba. According to his family, however, he was hit by another aircraft during a night mission. In any case, officially credited with 18 air kills, Wehmeyer was posthumously awarded the Knight's Cross, on September 4, 1942. One of the other two pilots killed was a veteran, Ofw. Otto Polenz, a former member of the Condor Legion who had recently returned two kills on the same day. On June 2, the recce Staffel 2.(H)/14 also suffered a serious loss when the Bf 110 E-3 flown by Staka Hptm. Hubert von Kühlwetter was shot down by antiaircraft artillery near Alusk. He was posthumously promoted to major.

The Luftwaffe would be tied up over Bir Hakeim for more than two weeks. LG 1 kept up heavy raids on British positions during the first 10 days of June but, very quickly, its Ju 88s were assigned to major convoy attacks and could no longer support the Afrika Korps directly. The same was true for II./KG 100 which had lost a number of He 111s over North Africa.

The German fighter arm once again proved its worth over North Africa as C. Shores explained:

> The Western Desert Air Force threw in everything to slow the Axis forces. Again the German fighters had a field day, taking a savage toll of the fighter-bombers ... Always refusing to get involved in dogfights with the escorting Kittyhawks and Tomahawks, the German pilots were content to sit up above and pick off the escorts, the British fighters units often being practically decimated.

However, where the German fighters failed was in dealing with Allied bombers—they never prevented them from carrying out their missions. An example of the rate at which German fighter pilot tallies were rising at that time can be seen in Oblt. Marseille's exploit on 17 June 1942: he claimed five kills, to bring his score to 101. At the same time the Stuka and Jabo units were being cut to pieces by Allied fighters. If, indeed, serious losses did occur within the *Schlacht* units (ground support), claims for Stukas shot down were often exaggerated, as these aircraft were far more robust than the Allies gave them credit for.

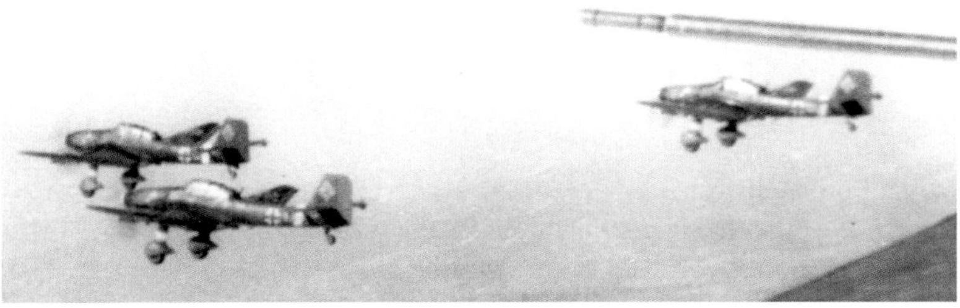

The Ju 87 Stuka force would be active in the capture of Tobruk but lost a number of aircraft.

But while Marseille went home to Berlin to receive the Oak Leaves and Swords, awarded respectively on June 6 and 18, JG 27 lost several quality pilots, including Oblt. Otto Schulz (4./JG 27) reported missing in action on June 17 near Sidi Rezegh. A 51-kill ace, he had been awarded the Knight's Cross on February 22, 1942.

By June 20, Rommel had decided to launch an all-out and ultimately decisive assault, taking advantage of the weakness of the British forces at the time. Most of the Ju 88 crews of LG 1 flew at least four sorties that day; their comrades in other units were not left out either. On the evening of June 21, the fortress of Tobruk was finally taken after fierce ground fighting. Later, Rommel, promoted to field marshal, visited various airfields to congratulate the airmen, and shake their hands, emphasizing their role in this great triumph of German arms.

The Luftwaffe had largely supported the ground forces in their advance and in the capture of Tobruk. In Malta, the Luftwaffe enjoyed some success but was beginning to suffer as Spitfires began arriving on the island in large numbers. As a result, the RAF/FAA (Fleet Air Arm) on Malta gradually upped its attacks on Axis maritime traffic. Again the question arose: Malta or Cairo? The freshly promoted Feldmarschall Rommel favored the push to

A collection of wrecks in the desert. The second Bf 10 "white 12" displays the badge of II./JG 3 and must be one of the few machines of 6./JG 3 lost in April 1942 in Libya. In the background, note the Ju 87, coded T6, a former II./St. G. 2 Stuka (now III./St.G. 3).

Egypt, although the Afrika Korps, exhausted by weeks of fighting, no longer had sufficient manpower or resources. On the other hand, despite its defeat, the British army could now count on the support of its American ally with its impressive arsenal of matériel.

Toward Egypt

The weeks following the fall of Tobruk were to prove decisive for the fate of the Axis army in Africa. According to C. Shores: "Rommel's plan had been to halt on the Egyptian frontier while an airborne invasion of Malta was undertaken to secure his supply lines … Now, he decided instead to carry straight on to Suez." Ultimately, this would prove a fateful decision which was to lose the war in Africa. While this may be true, it is worth noting two points: 1) Rommel's fatal decision was his first: to launch an all-out offensive in 1941, an offensive that would divert to Africa those German resources that would have achieved more and proved more effective in Russia, and 2) that Operation *Herkules*, the plan to invade and subdue Malta, was—without the Germans knowing it—doomed to fail from the outset, given the information available from Ultra, and the weakness of the invasion force, including the few Regia Marina ships capable of protecting the beachhead that would have been established by German airborne forces.

From late June to October 22, the Luftwaffe would face an unending war of attrition, constantly worn down by a British army in Egypt, with shortened supply lines and benefiting from an ever-increasing supply of American equipment.

An Initially Promising Offensive

As the frontlines moved rapidly eastward, so Luftwaffe units were forced to shift too. The Bf 110s of III./ZG 26 increasingly used airfields on Crete, such as Heraklion and Kastelli, that were less exposed to night raids by Wellington bombers. The *Zerstörer* were thus better able to escort the formations of Ju 52s bringing vital equipment to the Afrika Korps.

On June 26, major clashes took place at the gates of Mersa Matruh. JG 27 committed the lion's share of the effort to cover the German armored vanguard. III./JG 53 returned three kills that day but the Gruppe was surprised by a raid on Sidi Barrani airfield. At least

With British bombers based in Malta intensifying their night attacks on Sicily's airfields, I./NJG 2 sent Ju 88 Cs back to the island on June 23, leaving only four aircraft in North Africa.

Following the reinforcement of British antiaircraft defenses in Egypt, 2.(F)/123 was assigned a number of Ju 86 P twin-engined aircraft with pressurized cockpits, allowing it to fly over Suez and Alexandria at a higher altitude than the usual Ju 88s. Despite this, two of these aircraft were lost on operations.

seven of the unit's Bf 109s were destroyed as enemy bombers arrived overhead just as the "Pik As" fighters were in the midst of refueling. One pilot was killed and several others wounded.

With the situation on Malta improving for the defenders, the majority of the Ju 88 Cs of I./NJG 2 left for Sicily, leaving only four twin-engined aircraft in Africa to defend the ports. On June 29, Mersa Matruh fell. However, by that stage, the Axis forces in Africa were rapidly running out of steam even as they knocked at the doors of Egypt. The Luftwaffe in North Africa would henceforth operate primarily in two sectors: the British defensive line in Egypt by day and night; and, at night, over Suez and Alexandria with its bombers.

On the night of July 2/3, I. and II./LG 1 were airborne to mine the Suez Canal. During the return, a Ju 88 of 5./LG 1 had to carry out an emergency landing. On July 3, Lehrgeschwader 1 was subordinated to the Fliegerführer Afrika under General Otto Hoffmann von Waldau. Attacks on the El Alamein defensive line could thus be better coordinated.

On the night of July 3/4, II./KG 100 attacked airfields south of Alexandria. One of its He 111s was badly shot up by 87 Squadron but managed to limp back to Greece despite serious damage. On July 4, as German fighters escalated their missions, JG 27 suffered a severe blow with the loss of Lt. Friedrich Körner (2./JG 27) who was shot down near El Alamein and captured. He had returned more than 30 kills in a year of fighting in the desert. On the same day, Rommel temporarily halted the ground attacks against the British line to give his soldiers some rest and reorganize his forces. This did not prevent LG 1 from continuing its

On July 4, 1942 JG 27 lost one of its great aces, Lt. Friedrich Körner, but other JG 27 aces continued to increase their tallies, such as the Austrian Oblt. Rudolf Sinner (6./JG 27), seen here flanked by his two mechanics on the wing of his Bf 109 F.

In Profile:
Transport aircraft

Fw 200 Condor C-3 of 9./KG 40.

Ju 52/3m of 2./KGzbV 1 temporarily assigned to KGzbV 400.

Me 323D-1 of 1./KGzbV 323.

Oblt. Franz Götz of JG 53 earned his Knight's Cross in the fierce fighting over the Egyptian border and would not be the only one to do so.

missions by often using Fouka as an intermediate base. Later that evening, however, it recorded some heavy losses: over Suez, 3./LG 1 lost a Ju 88 shot down by a nightfighter, and two crews, from 4. and 5./LG 1, failed to return to Crete, having been shot down by antiaircraft fire.

On July 5, I. and II. and II./LG 1 took off from Heraklion to bomb targets near El Alamein. The Ju 88s landed at Bir el Abd. A little later, 3./LG 1 was ordered to conduct an armed reconnaissance on Burg el Arab. The Ju 88s orbiting the aerodrome to form up were then surprised by Kittyhawks of 450 Squadron RAAF. One German twin, landing late, was surprised, probably as the aircraft was virtually out of fuel, and shot down. There were no survivors. Three Ju 88s were seriously damaged on the ground and successive fighter-bomber attacks forced them to return to Crete. Despite this episode, the Ju 88s set out for El Alamein in the afternoon, continuing their reconnaissance and bombing missions, but this time all returning to Heraklion, with some putting down to refuel at Bir el Abd.

On the night of July 6/7, during a series of mining and bombing operations in the Suez Canal area, two II./KG 100 aircraft were shot down by a Beaufighter of 46 Squadron The next day, another canal-mining mission resulted in the loss of a 6./KG 100 He 111. Another Heinkel was shot down near Burg el Arab in an airfield attack. On July 9, as Rommel launched his first major offensive, LG 1 was deployed in support but could not prevent the Australian

To weaken the Luftwaffe, raids against German airfields were mounted, not only from the air but also by the SAS and the Long Range Desert Group operating in small units in all-terrain vehicles. On July 27, one such an attack, on Quasaba, proved successful.

A LG 1 Ju 88 being readied for a night mission.

9th Infantry Division from inflicting heavy losses on the Italian Sabratha Division. On July 11, the panzers fought ferociously to plug the gaps and increasing numbers of sorties were flown by the Ju 88s, with one LG 1 machine falling to antiaircraft fire.

The Bf 109s of JG 27 and III./JG 53 were increasingly coming up against Spitfires, with which 145 Squadron, among others, was equipped. As over Malta, these modern fighters—more so than the Hurricane and Kittyhawk—would prove difficult opponents for the *Tagjäger*. While the Luftwaffe continued to rack up successes, they were increasingly difficult to achieve.

July 11 saw an attack by 13 Beaufighters on a Ju 52 formation approaching the African coast. The three-engined transports were being escorted by only a Bf 110, a Ju 88, and an He 111. Three Ju 52s were claimed but two Beaufighters were forced to make emergency landings. This was one of the many attacks aimed at disrupting Axis fuel resupply operations by using Ultra intelligence. III./ZG 26, which regularly conduced Jabo operations over the desert, could only be deployed piecemeal, its *Zerstörer* being most often used as shipping or Ju 52 transport escorts. Fighters on both sides were not idle despite planes lost or rendered unserviceable by sand and heat. Pilots, on the other hand, very often suffered from illness, malaria and other fevers. Refueling continued to be ad hoc. Despite all this, on July 14, German fighters flew no fewer than 127 sorties. Three days later, they flew another 166 sorties.

On the night of July 14/15, British tanks launched a powerful assault in the Ruweisat area, forcing 12./LG 1 to intervene to support the two LG 1 Gruppen. On July 17, the fighting was so fierce that about 20 Bf 109s of II./JG 53 left Comiso to support the remainder of III./

On July 15, 1942 Hptm. Kurt Kuhlmey, leading II./St. G. 3, received the Knight's Cross from his superior, Obstlt. Walter Sigel. Throughout the North African campaign, the robust Ju 87s operated tirelessly. In April 1943, Kuhlmey succeeded Sigel.

A Ju 88 being overhauled.

JG 53 still present at Quotaifiya. However, to maintain some pressure on Malta, II./JG 53 departed for Sicily three days later. On July 20, the RAF carried out major attacks on Fuka and El Daba airfields with bombers and fighters equipped with bombs. A Ju 88 of I./LG 1 was destroyed at Bir el Abd. In the afternoon, LG 1 returned the courtesy by bombing Alam el Mireibat airfield.

On July 22, despite increasing losses, ground activity did not slack off. LG 1 flew into Haga el Quasaba to conduct dive-bombing attacks against El Ruweisat before returning to Crete. Fighting was intense and, on that day, Oblt. Franz Götz of 9./JG 53 returned his 40th kill: a 601 Squadron Spitfire. This earned him the Knight's Cross that he did not receive until September 4.

On July 23, the Luftwaffe mounted a major operation: the Bf 110s of III./ZG 26 were committed and, exceptionally, no fewer than 19 machines were launched to escort 30 Ju 52/3m transports carrying an infantry battalion to occupy the Siwa oasis. This effort was largely in vain since the oasis had been evacuated a short time earlier by British forces. But prevention was better than cure, as local Luftwaffe commanders had bad memories of the May 12 massacre of the

In front of a KGzbV 1 aircraft. Like all passengers to Africa, this member of the Ramcke Brigade has donned a *Schwimmveste*, a life vest, for the flight over the Mediterranean.

Ramcke Brigade troops board Ju 52s.

The Ramcke Brigade

The capture of Fortress Tobruk did not, of course, put an end to the war in the desert. A much-depleted Afrika Korps had to be rebuilt as soon as possible, despite this resounding success. Reinforcements were thus dispatched in haste, aggravating the problem of supplies. One unit that arrived in Libya at the time was the Luftwaffenjäger-Brigade 1, which would earn the nickname "Ramcke Brigade" after paratroop commander Major General Bernhard Ramcke, a leading airborne figure and a veteran of the Crete campaign of May 1941 (for which he received the Knight's Cross). "Papa" Ramcke began his career during World War I, serving in the Marinekorps in Flanders. Like the sailors of 1916, the Brigade paratroopers also served as infantrymen. The Fallschirm-Brigade was to assemble elements of pioneers, artillery, and antitank guns. These Fallschirmjäger were to face off against the British defensive line at El Alamein, but, during the British offensive of October 23, were to suffer the full weight of the attack. Surrounded, they managed to capture an Eighth Army supply column, thus enabling them to return to their lines on November 7. However, when they reassembled at Fuka, the 4,000 men initially sent to Africa had been whittled down to six hundred.

Despite the difficulties, Ramcke was able to bring the remnants of his brigade back to Tunisia to take part in the final battles, an exploit for which he received the Oak Leaves.

Ju 52s, as well as many other attacks against vulnerable Ju 52 formations.

II./KG 100 continued to operate against Suez installations as well as fuel depots near the canal. On the night of July 27/28, an He 111 of the Gruppe was shot down by 46 Squadron. On the night of July 30/31, near Abukir, another 46 Squadron aircraft shot down an He 111 that had taken off from Kalamaki to bomb Heluan airfield. As a result of these losses, II./KG 100's aircraft strength dwindled to just five serviceable aircraft.

Major General Ramcke decorates several soldiers.

Ramcke chats to a relaxed Erwin Rommel.

August 1942: Stalemate

August saw a similar war of attrition to that of July's but the extent of the clashes in the air was such that, on August 6, bled white, III./ZG 26 was transferred back to Crete for rest and refit. Henceforth the Bf 110s were divided between Sicily and Greece, carrying out maritime patrols, Ju 52 transport or bomber escort missions during convoy attacks. As K. Gundelach points out, in August 1942, a third of Luftwaffe aircraft and personnel in the Mediterranean were operating on convoy protection duties. This high figure proves that, little by little, the German air force was moving from an offensive to a defensive position even though its fighter aircraft continued to see intense action over the desert. To compensate for the withdrawal of the Bf 110s from North Africa, the Fliegerführer Afrika was bolstered with another arrival from the Soviet Union—III./ZG 1, a ground support unit equipped with Bf 109 Es.

In Profile:
Hauptmann Roland Borth

In September 1939 Roland Borth was an Oberleutnant and a Bf 109 D pilot in JGr. 152, one of a number of small day fighter units disbanded early in 1940. On September 24, 1939, during a clash with Curtiss H-75s of GC I/3 of the Armée de l'Air, his "Dora" was shot down near Bettviller (Sarreguemines) and he was captured by the French. His injuries were such that it was believed he would never fly again. However, freed nine months later when France fell, he had recovered sufficiently to lead 9./ZG 26, a Bf 110 Staffel, following his appointment as Hauptmann. An amazing conversion, it was not his only one, as in late April 1941 he was posted to the Schlacht arm. In early 1942, he took over as head of the newly established III./ZG 1, operating the Bf 109 E in the USSR. In August, III./ZG 1 was transferred to Africa. Borth was shot down near El Alamein on September 1, 1942 and died of his injuries eight days later.

Hptm. Roland Borth, on his successful return from his 100th combat sortie in Russia, is feted by his comrades in front of his Bf 109 Emil.

Uffz. Werner "Stumpen" Stumpf of 9./JG 53 received the Knight's Cross on August 13, 1942 for his 40 kills. He added eight more before being killed in action on October 13, 1942.

Bombers based in Greece continued their missions mainly over Egypt. On the night of August 1/2, LG 1 set out again to bomb targets near El Alamein. During the sorties mounted during the night of August 2/3, the He 111 carrying the Staka of 4./KG 100 failed to return from a flight south of Alexandria.

German bombing operations were disrupted on August 10. In order to resupply Malta, under heavy Luftwaffe pressure, the Royal Navy launched Operation *Pedestal*, a convoy of 13 cargo ships and a very well-escorted tanker destined for the island. Ju 88s and He 111s escorted by Bf 109s and 110s operated for several days against these ships, being thus forced, by necessity, to abandon North Africa. Even if the front remained stable, fighters from both sides continued to clash, with fighter-bombers being widely deployed by both sides. On August 13, news arrived at JG 53 headquarters breaking the monotony of war. Uffz. Werner Stumpf of 9. Staffel had been honored with the Knight's Cross for his 40 kills. However, he would only wear it for a short time.

On August 15, ack-ack fire brought down Ogfr. Werner Staudt's 10.(Jabo)/JG 53 Bf 109 during a Jabo raid over the Ruweisat area. This is the last official mention of the Jabo-Staffel of the "Pik As." On August 31, this unit was included in the brand-new "Jabogruppe Afrika," command of which was handed over to Hptm. Werner Langemann, formerly Staka of 10./JG 53. On August 20, Lt. Hans-Arnold Stahlschmidt, a veteran of 2./JG 27 and a close friend of ace Hans-Joachim Marseille, also received the Knight's Cross for his 48 kills. But, like Stumpf of the "Pik As," he would only wear it for a short time.

Operation *Pedestal* having ended, the bombers returned to Egypt. On the night of August 21/22, II./LG 1 bombed Alexandria. A Ju 88 fell victim to 46 Squadron. On the way back to base, one aircraft crashed at El Quasaba. The following night saw an attack by I./LG 1 against El Mirbat airfield near Alexandria. On the night of August 23/24, II./LG 1, dispatched against Alexandria again, lost a Ju 88 shot down by 89 Squadron. On the evening of August 24, I./LG 1 flew sorties against Bir Hooker aerodrome. 73 Squadron shot down one of the Ju 88s engaged near Burg el Arab. On the night of August 28/29, elements of I./LG 1 flew into Berca in order to bomb British positions at El Alamein. The next day, the Ju 88s returned

JG 27 saw continuous action in the desert. Knight's Cross recipient and Kommander of I./JG 27 since June 1942, Hptm Gerhard Homuth's aircraft displays his many kills.

to Heraklion. On the same night, more Ju 88s attacked Bir Hooker airfield, losing an aircraft to Hurricanes south of Alexandria. The next day, I. Gruppe attacked aerodromes around Alexandria.

In the early morning of August 31, Rommel went over to the offensive again, but the Panzerarmee Afrika encountered stiff British defenses, including minefields. The Axis forces were pushed back after a few days. In the evening, LG 1 bombed enemy positions in the El Alamein area.

Hptm. Werner Langemann, leader of 10.(Jabo)/JG 53, took command of a new Jabo unit in August, the "Jabogruppe Afrika." It only existed for a few weeks.

Despite its successes, the *Tagjagd* was being constantly worn down. On August 21, 1942, Lt. Gerhard Mix of 6./JG 27 was shot down and had to land his Bf 109 F-4/Trop near El Alamein. He was taken captive while his machine was placed under guard.

On August 23, 1942, 2.(F)/123 based at Kastelli (Crete) celebrated its 2,000th *Feindflug* (combat sortie). A large number of them were carried out over Egypt at the cost of several losses.

A Bf 109 of III./ZG 1 lost in Libya. This unit, which arrived in the desert in August, was to be recalled at the end of September to convert onto the Me 210.

1942: End of an Era

On September 1, LG 1 continued with its missions in support of the ground forces but the Italian-German offensive stalled. III./ZG 1 lost its Kommandeur that day. On September 3, a British counteroffensive in Alam el Halfa pushed the attackers back to their start lines. The Ju 88s of LG 1 were in action again but three Ju 88s were damaged on landing at Hagag el Quasaba. On the night of September 3/4, during an attack on the British defensive line, a Junkers was shot down by a 46 Squadron Beaufighter. On September 4, even though Oberbefehlshaber Süd, Feldmarschall Albert Kesselring, visited Heraklion to express his displeasure following the heavy losses suffered by the Luftwaffe, by September 6, the battle of Alam el Halfa had ended. This was the last Italian-German attempt to reach the Suez Canal. It is noteworthy that during the war in the air American P-40 F and B-25 aircraft were used extensively, confirming American involvement in what was gradually becoming a "material war."

In the meantime, the Ju 88 Cs of I./NJG 2 that were shared between Sicily and Africa were recalled to Belgium. The RAF's night attacks on the Reich were increasing and these aircraft were considered more useful in European skies. The defense of Libya's airfields was therefore left to fall mainly on the Flak arm.

On September 2, Obstlt. Walter Sigel, who had brilliantly led Stukageschwader 3 in combat, received the Oak Leaves. The next day, another Stuka pilot, Oblt. Martin Mossdorf, Kapitän of 3./St.G. 3, was finally awarded the Knight's Cross. But it was not all success and decorations. On September 7, JG

Obstlt. Walter Sigel, Kommodore of St. G. 3, received the Oak Leaves in September 1942 in recognition of his unit's successes.

In an effort to strengthen the precarious Afrika Korps supply situation, gliders were deployed, such as this 1. (DFS)/VK (S) 2 DFS 230. During the British offensive, many had to be abandoned.

On September 7, 1942, Lt. Stahlschmidt disappeared in action. The loss of this ace was keenly felt by JG 27. Here "Fifi" Stahlschmidt (second from right) chats with another JG 27 ace, Lt. Werner Schroer (left).

On September 30, Stahlschmidt's comrade, Hptm. "Jochen" Marseille, was killed bailing out of a new Bf 109 G-2.

Marseille was given a lavish funeral.

27 suffered a bitter blow with the loss of Lt. Hans-Arnold Stahlschmidt in combat. “Fifi” Stahlschmidt went down about 30 kilometers from El Alamein. A close friend of Jochen Marseille, he was one of the first to arrive with I./JG 27 in Africa and was credited with 60 kills. He would posthumously receive the Oak Leaves.

With the Axis blocked in their positions, the emboldened British were becoming increasingly aggressive. On September 14, a combined operation was organized targeting Tobruk but intervention by the Ju 87s of III./St. G. 3 largely helped to defeat it. The cruiser HMS *Coventry*, seriously damaged by Stuka bombs, had to be scuttled by its escort.

Still, the Luftwaffe managed to operate relentlessly, whether against the defensive positions around El Alamein or against enemy shipping. On September 24, Oblt. Herbert Stry, the Staffelkapitän of 5./St.G. 3, was awarded the Knight’s Cross after more than 300 combat sorties. Acts of courage were noted. On September 25, during an attack on the Koufra oasis, an He 111 of II./KG 100 was forced to land in the desert. A fellow pilot landed his machine nearby, loaded up the crew and returned to Kalamaki with eight men on board. Despite such individual efforts, the Luftwaffe was being insidiously reduced.

September 30 was a black day for the Luftwaffe: that great ace of the desert campaign, Hptm. “Jochen” Marseille, Kapitän of 3./JG 27, was killed attempting to bail out of his machine, a recently delivered Bf 109 G-2/Trop, the latest variant of the Bf 109 that was still suffering from teething problems. Returning from an uneventful sortie, his engine suffered a failure and the cockpit started to fill with smoke. Marseille rolled the fighter over on its back, jettisoned the canopy and dropped clear. But he struck the tailfin and was knocked out, plunging to the ground near Abd el Rahman. Credited with 158 kills, the “Star of Africa” thus perished, undefeated. Strangely enough, his death seemed to mark the end of the “good times” for the Luftwaffe in Africa, much as if there was a “before” and an “after” Marseille. From that moment on, events accelerated and would now turn completely against the Axis forces. At the end of September, III./ZG 1 (which had lost its Kommandeur) and Jabogruppe Afrika (which had existed for only a few weeks) were withdrawn from the front to form a new ground support unit, Schlachtgeschwader 2. But, if the Jabogruppe became I./SG 2, III./ZG 1 remained independent while re-equipping with the Me 210.

Feldmarschall Kesselring, OB Süd, was present at Marseille's burial.

The beginning of October saw heavy rains. In preparation for the upcoming British offensive, the Desert Air Force aircraft attempted large-scale raids against Axis airfields to break the back of the enemy air forces. Despite this, the Luftwaffe and Regia Aeronautica were able to inflict serious losses on the attackers, albeit at a cost. On October 13, Ofw. Werner Stumpf, one of the leading aces of III./JG 53, with 47 kills, was shot down and killed. Like Stahlschmidt, he had only briefly worn his Knight's Cross.

On October 2, I./JG 27 was withdrawn from the North African theater due to its losses and the state of exhaustion of its personnel. But it was not to benefit from any rest. Having collected new "Gustavs" at Bari, the pilots were sent to Sicily to fly sorties over Malta. However, due to lack of resources, I./JG 27 achieved little against the Spitfires now equipping the squadrons defending Malta.

On October 23, after lengthy preparations, having been strongly reinforced, the Eighth Army, now led by Lieutenant General Bernard Montgomery launched the fresh British offensive, what would be known as the second battle of El Alamein. Montgomery's numerical superiority in tanks and artillery was impressive. The same applied to his air force. In the Middle East, Allied air forces could draw on some 1,500 aircraft. Facing them Luftflotte 2 could only line up 914 machines, of which only 528 were serviceable. At the front itself, the Western Desert Air Force had assembled some 530 aircraft, against which the Italians and Germans could only field 324 aircraft, 167 of which were airworthy. The *Tagjagd*, consisting of JG 27 and III./JG 53, exhausted by weeks of intense fighting, weakened by the loss of many of its aces, was particularly weak, virtually bled white.

The cross on the tomb of the "Star of Africa." Marseille was re-interred in the German cemetery at Tobruk.

Retreat

October 23, 1942 was a fateful date for the Axis army in Africa—Montgomery launched his Eighth Army into the decisive offensive at El Alamein. The fighting would rage across the front, which had remained almost static up until then. Bf 110 and Ju 88 twins of III./ZG 26 were urgently recalled to Africa in an attempt to slow the irresistible advance of the British forces, this at a time when they were required to provide the necessary escort cover over the supply routes of the hard-pressed Axis forces. For its part, I./JG 27, then based in Sicily, returned to Africa with the greatest possible speed.

Reinforcements for the Luftwaffe in Africa

In view of the attrition sustained by JG 27, it had already been planned to replace the Geschwader with JG 77, which had previously operated in Russia. III./JG 77 arrived in Munich on October 16 from the Leningrad area. Brand-new Bf 109 G-2s (trop) were waiting for them and by October 23/24, III./JG 77 was already arriving on a stopover in Bari. On October 25/26, I./JG 77, which had been operating in Sicily for weeks, stopped over in Tripoli before leaving for Benghazi.

With all available German aircraft engaged on the El Alamein front, efforts to subdue Malta eased and convoy escorts could no longer be assured. On October 26, despite the presence of at least one Ju 88 of 2./LG 1, a convoy of Axis ships was attacked near Tobruk by a large formation of bombers, sinking the cargo vessel *Tergestia* and the oil tanker *Proserpina*. This

During the British offensive on October 23, 1942, Feldmarschall Rommel was on leave in Germany. Returning urgently, he stopped over on October 25 in Heraklion (Crete) and held talks with General Friedrich-Wilhelm Müller (commander of the 22nd Infantry Division stationed in Crete—on the left of Rommel) and General Otto Hoffmann von Waldau (Fliegerführer Afrika—extreme right) before reaching Tobruk.

Luftflotte 2 strength return October 20, 1942

	Total aircraft (serviceable)	Aircraft subordinated to Fl.F. Afrika (serviceable)
Battlefield reconnaissance	11 (10)	11 (10)
Strategic reconnaissance	51 (28)	5 (3)
Fighters	200 (123)	104 (58)
Zerstörer (Bf 110)	69 (28)	69 (28)
Fighter bombers (Jabo)	55 (27)	55 (27)
Bombers	225 (129)	
Dive bombers (Stuka)	112 (65)	80 (41)
Maritime aircraft	11 (8)	
Transports	180 (110) resupply to Africa	

Note

- The African front has drawn in more than half of the fighters in L.Fl. 2, leaving relatively few machines in Sicily to face the Spitfires based on Malta.
- All III./ZG 26 was deployed on the El Alamein front at the expense of convoy escort duties.
- Two-thirds of all Ju 87 Stukas were deployed over Africa and were no longer available for missions over Malta.
- Bombers could now only operate from Crete or Sicily, being to susceptible to RAF and SAS/LRDG strikes in the desert.

was a real disaster for the Afrika Korps, whose panzers' overriding requirement was fuel. On October 26, 1942, III./JG 77 departed Italy for North Africa, via Greece and Crete, final destination Tobruk. En route, the pilots were left under no illusions as to the difficulties that awaited them there. Ofw. "Edu" Isken (8./JG 77) recalled:

> We made a refueling stop in Athens. The airfield commander invited us in for a coffee, one of the first decent cups of coffee we had drunk for a while. Then we were airborne again, heading for Crete and Tobruk. We had barely overflown the island when a huge column of smoke could be made out. Enemy torpedo bombers had just sunk a munitions freighter close to the port of Tobruk. We landed a short while later, my Schwarm being the very first unit of the Gruppe to arrive in North Africa. We spent our first night in wrecked vehicles. The next day we were introduced to a senior officer. He immediately declared that the African campaign was lost. And we would lose it even quicker now, as the previous day the Luftwaffe had failed to stop enemy torpedo bombers from sinking a cargo freighter loaded with munitions. It was difficult not to think back to the cup of coffee that had delayed us by a quarter of an hour and probably prevented us from intercepting the ship's attackers.

A pilot of III./JG 77 photographed his unit's Bf 109 Gustavs on their flight from Crete to Tobruk.

Elements of III./JG 77 were assigned to other duties as the Kapitän 7./JG 77 and Knight's Cross recipient Hptm. Dieter Huy related:

> I left Bari heading for Taormina with four aircraft to be subordinated to the Fliegerkorps. For a few days we headed out in the direction of Crete on convoy escort duty. As a former Seeflieger in the naval air arm, I had flown these types of sorties before. Field Marshal Albert Kesselring arrived in Chania and I introduced myself. It was the first time that I had met him. Despite the difference in age and rank between us, he appeared friendly and jovial, even inviting me to a meeting on the situation in Africa. I learned that we were short of fuel and that it had to be brought in on Italian cruisers across the Mediterranean. He did not hide the precarious nature of our situation. The African campaign was lost. Soon afterward I reached Africa with my four fighters and was welcomed by JG 27 in the same tent that had belonged to Hans-Joachim Marseille.

The newcomers were immediately thrown into the fray. On October 27, I./JG 77 left Tripoli for Bir-el-Abd, a few kilometers from El Alamein. III./JG 77 moved onto the airfield at Tanyet-Harun. During a reconnaissance flight with his wingman, Ofw. Herbert Kaiser (8./JG 77) flew over the Via Balbia before seeing six P-40s strafing the road. Kaiser shot down two of them but was himself the victim of a third. With his machine on fire, Kaiser managed to make a belly-landing in the desert. He then had to walk four long hours before reaching the road. Two days later, he met up again with his comrades who already considered him dead. One of the first aces of III./JG 77 to be lost was Hptm. Huy. This 40-kill veteran had immediately noticed the differences in the fighting:

> In Russia combat rarely took place at altitudes higher than 4,000 meters and only in small groups of five to ten aircraft. On the African continent, sorties were flown at very high altitudes (minimum 6,000 meters) to the point

On October 28, Hptm. Wolf-Dieter Huy, a III./JG 77 veteran who had been fighting since the beginning of the war, was shot down and captured.

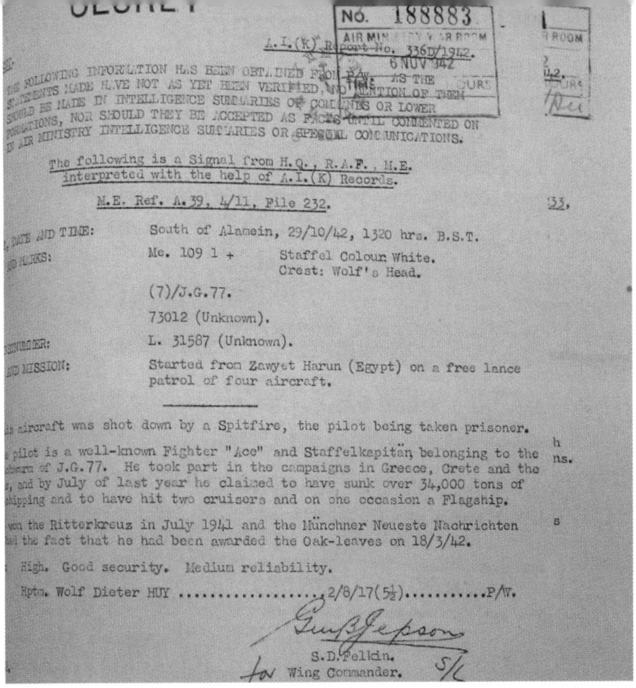

SECRET

NO. 188883

AIR MINISTRY WAR ROOM

A.I.(K) Report No. 336D/1942.

6 NOV 1942

THE FOLLOWING INFORMATION HAS BEEN OBTAINED FROM P/W. AS THE STATEMENTS MADE HAVE NOT AS YET BEEN VERIFIED, NO MENTION OF THEM SHOULD BE MADE IN INTELLIGENCE SUMMARIES OF COMMANDS OR LOWER FORMATIONS, NOR SHOULD THEY BE ACCEPTED AS FACTS UNTIL COMMENTED ON IN AIR MINISTRY INTELLIGENCE SUMMARIES OR SPECIAL COMMUNICATIONS.

The following is a Signal from H.Q., R.A.F., M.E. interpreted with the help of A.I.(K) Records.

M.E. Ref. A.39, 4/11, File 232.

DATE AND TIME: South of Alamein, 29/10/42, 1320 hrs. B.S.T.

MARKS: Me. 109 1 + Staffel Colour White. Crest: Wolf's Head.

(7)/J.G.77.

73012 (Unknown).

NUMBER: L. 31587 (Unknown).

AND MISSION: Started from Zawyet Harun (Egypt) on a free lance patrol of four aircraft.

This aircraft was shot down by a Spitfire, the pilot being taken prisoner.

The pilot is a well-known Fighter "Ace" and Staffelkapitän belonging to the ... of J.G.77. He took part in the campaigns in Greece, Crete and the ..., and by July of last year he claimed to have sunk over 34,000 tons of shipping and to have hit two cruisers and on one occasion a Flagship.

... won the Ritterkreuz in July 1941 and the Münchner Neueste Nachrichten ... the fact that he had been awarded the Oak-leaves on 18/3/42.

High. Good security. Medium reliability.

Hptm. Wolf Dieter HUY ....2/8/17(5½)..........P/W.

S.D. Felkin.
for Wing Commander.

This brief report of Huy's capture has a concise and accurate account of his career.

that often the yellow of the coast and the blue sea under our wings stood out as if we were contemplating a map (this led to great difficulties finding our airfield). The formations of aircraft were larger and it was not uncommon to face groups of forty or more bombers with fighter escort. On October 28, I was returning from a sortie when I was attacked by Spitfires. I was wounded in the arm and my ship rapidly caught alight, leaving me with little chance to defend myself. I had to bail out for the first time. I jettisoned the canopy. Although the aircraft was out of control, I was able to jump clear at around 8,000 meters. The thin air caused me to pass out at 5,000 meters.

I came to on the ground to find myself facing two Greek soldiers belonging to the Sacred Battalion [Note:the Hellenic detachment of the British Army, the Sacred Battalion, had not yet been created]. They took me to their doctor, who had studied in Heidelberg and spoke very good German. He treated my burns. I was then handed over to the British, who took my medals (including my Knight's Cross) while giving me a receipt. Subsequently, the medal case was lost and although I kept hold of my receipt, I never got back my decorations! I was sent to the hospital at Geneifa and then interned in a camp in Egypt. In 1943, still considered severely wounded, there was talk of exchanging me via the International Red Cross but this came to nothing and I remained in captivity until the end of the war.

Fhj-Uffz. Hans-Werner Renzow of 8./JG 77 recalled:

The situation in Africa was dire; the numerical superiority of the enemy was on average ten to one! Our combat experience was our only advantage. Indeed, many of us arrived from Russia with a good track record while our opponents had yet to be tested in combat. And while we had sufficient supplies, the quality was lacking. However, no one died of hunger. Worst of all was the shortage of drinking water. Our filters were not effective. The water and, therefore the coffee, always had a salty taste. We would thus avoid this filtered water. On the other hand we always managed to procure fuel: our aircraft were too important to do without. Despite these conditions, our losses were relatively light. As for myself, I only had to make a single parachute jump. On November 15, 1942 I was scrambled with Heinz Lüdemann to

Faced with the powerful Eighth Army attack, Axis forces buckled and fell back. This column of paratroopers from the surrounded Ramcke Brigade would nevertheless return to its lines.

A Ju 88 of LG 1 was shot down during the clashes over El Alamein.

> intercept three unescorted Viermots approaching our base. As we closed on them, they changed heading. We set off in pursuit. Soon afterward, black smoke began to stream from my comrade's machine and he was forced to turn back. My radio was not working that day but I decided to continue alone. Young and unthinking that I was! I caught the bombers and sent one down in flames. It sank at sea some forty to fifty kilometers from our base. In the second attack, my aircraft was hit and caught fire. With my face and arms burnt, I had to parachute clear. Aside from the chute, a dinghy was also attached to my back. In contact with water, it partially inflated, leaving me to finish blowing it up. I hoisted myself aboard. The wind and the sun dried my clothes but my burns, made more painful by the salt, made me suffer. I was adrift at sea for three days: from November 15 to 17. On the morning of November 17, I finally saw the coast. I jumped out of the boat, hoping to swim to the mainland. This quickly proved impossible and I had great difficulty in getting back into my dinghy. The wind became my ally and pushed me toward the coast. However, this took all day. Exhausted and hungry I fell onto the beach and went straight to sleep. An Arab discovered me during the night. He took me to his camp and gave me food. After one night there, an Italian motorcyclist took me back to my unit where they had given me up for dead. I was granted leave and returned to Germany. I was awarded the Iron Cross second class soon afterward and I received the EK 1 [Eisernes Kreuz 1, or Iron Cross first class] for my twelfth kill.

On November 2, Montgomery initiated Operation *Supercharge* that opened a breach in the Italian–German front. LG 1 flew increasing numbers of sorties that also included an unsuccessful search for a submarine and even a reconnaissance mission in the direction of Alexandria. Over the following 48 hours, the Afrika Korps began its retreat to Fuka. The Ju 88s of LG 1 were split between convoy escort missions and night-fighting sorties.

In view of the seriousness of the situation, the Luftwaffe high command assembled everything it could scrape together, often in a very eclectic way: on November 2, Oblt. Julius Meimberg, Staffelkapitän of 11 (Höhe) /JG 2, was summoned by his superior officer, Kommodore Walter Oesau. According to his recollections:

> He had some news he had to share with me. "Meimberg," he told me in his inimitable style, "for you and the eleventh Staffel, there is change in the air. Take three Ju 52s, thirty men of the technical staff and as much equipment as the Junkers can carry and then go to North Africa." I was so stunned that I replied almost mechanically: "Jawohl, Herr Oberstleutnant! And where in North Africa? "The precise orders have yet to arrive. But first you will fly into Sicily via Munich."

Another high-altitude fighter Staffel, 11./JG 26, was also withdrawn from France to operate in Africa. All three Gruppen of JG 53 were sent to Africa. However, the Geschwader was in the midst of a reorganization. I./JG 53 still partially equipped with the Friedrich. II./JG 53 had detachments scattered at Araxos, Pantelleria, and Bari, while III./JG 53 had been largely deployed over Libya but had suffered losses and its pilots were exhausted. Parts of I./JG 53, in the process of being reconstituted, were sent to Libya. On November 2, a G-2 from 3./JG 53 was destroyed while landing at Tobruk. The departure from Sicily of the "Pik As" marked the end of operations to reduce Malta which once again would become an Allied strongpoint capable of seriously hindering Axis resupply operations to Africa.

On November 5, at Jesau, II./JG 51 returned from the Eastern Front to convert onto the Fw 190 and learned that they were being sent to Africa. The training course was immediately terminated for 4. and 5. /JG 51 who kept their Bf 109 G-2 fighters, enabling them to set out as soon as possible. However 6./JG 51 did replace its Bf 109s with Fw 190s and returned to the Eastern Front. According to one writer:

> The reaction to this news was very different within the two Staffeln concerned. The ground staff and many young pilots were happy not to have to spend another harsh winter in the USSR. But the "old hands" were more sceptical. They feared what would follow: long flights over the sea, hard dogfighting with Allied pilots, forced landings in the desert or in rugged terrain offering less chance of survival than putting down on a thick covering of snow in the USSR.

To complete this Gruppe, a new 6./JG 51 was created by renaming 3./JG 1 detached from its Geschwader. On November 7, the Bf 109s of I./SG 2 landed at Martuba from Sicily, further reducing the already negligible pressure on Malta. The Stab JG 77, led by Maj. Joachim Müncheberg, arrived late because it had to take possession of brand-new Bf 109 G-2 (trop) fighters. However at the time, Müncheberg only had two Gruppen because II./JG 77, still on the Eastern Front, did not begin its transfer until November 10. This new theater of war undoubtedly brought back memories for the Kommodore who, the previous year, had fought in Libya as Staka 7./JG 26.

Meanwhile, on the El Alamein front, Luftwaffe fighters still managed to achieve some notable successes, even as they were hunted down on the ground, not only by the Desert Air Force but by the United States Army Air Forces (USAAF) now deployed over North Africa. Lt. Armin Köhler of I./JG 77 noted in a diary entry dated November 3:

Two of the ground support pilots of I./SG 2 which arrived in Martuba on November 7, 1942: Lt. Wilhelm Vetter (l.) was reported missing over Africa on March 22, 1943 while Fw. Bernhard "Brummwieh" Johannes was killed at Kaunas on July 11, 1944. He was posthumously awarded the Knight's Cross.

In an attempt to compensate for the dramatic drop in maritime traffic between Europe and Africa, the Luftwaffe deployed the Me 323s of I./KGzbV 323 to supply the Tunisian bridgehead. The heavy *Giganten* were to suffer significant losses in 1943.

Operation *Torch*

Rommel ordered his forces to fall back in the hope, as previously, of recreating a line of defense when his enemy had overstretched his lines and in turn was experiencing supply problems. However, on the morning of November 8, the Allies commenced their landings in Morocco and Algeria—Operation *Torch*—trapping the Axis armies in a pincer. Although caught by surprise and still hoping to reinforce the Panzerarmee Afrika and its air force, the German high command reacted quickly by launching 118 bombers of the LG 1, KG 6, KG 54, KG 77, KG 26, KG 100, and III./KG 30 against the invasion force: the majority of the aircraft based in Sicily reinforced by aircraft from Greece. But this operation, which was hastily conceived and conducted in cloudy skies, was never likely to prove successful. On November 9, the bombers again mounted an operation against the invasion fleet off Algiers. II./LG 1 flew at night. A British supply ship, the *Palomares*, was reportedly damaged.

On their arrival in Algiers, the Americans discovered this He 111 in civilian markings on the airfield at Maison Blanche. It served with the Franco-German commission in charge of verifying the French army's compliance with the June 1940 armistice.

A Fallschirmjäger motorcycle unit arriving in Tunisia rides directly to the front, passing a column of camels.

Since Morocco and Algeria could not be taken back from the American–British forces, the OKW decided to occupy Tunisia as soon as possible. Airfields were secured by paratroops, and air units were directed toward this sector to block aircraft coming from the western Maghreb. To do so, it was necessary to force the hand of the Vichy authorities who governed the country.

To transport equipment and men as quickly as possible at a time when maritime transport was now largely threatened by Malta, the recently established I./KGzbV 323 equipped with Me 323 six-engined transports was dispatched to the Mediterranean. These *Giganten* (giants) were able to carry loads of up to 13 tons of equipment, mainly engine oil and fuel. On November 10, Beaufighters of 272 Squadron from Takali (Malta) strafed El Aouina, destroying several German aircraft, including an Me 323, the first *Gigant* lost in Africa. The machine was probably the victim of Sqn Ldr Anthony Watson who claimed "a large glider." I./KGzbV 323 remained temporarily at Lecce while using the Neapolitan Capodichino airfield as a forward base for its direct flights to Tunisia.

Throughout November, departures and arrivals followed one another in quick succession. On November 10, II./JG 77 departed the USSR to join the rest of the Geschwader in Africa. On November 12, the

Zum frommen Gedenken

an den Kriegsfreiwilligen

LOTHAR BEIL

Obergefreiter

in einem Fallschirmjäger-Regiment

geboren am 28. Januar 1921

gefallen am 26. Februar 1943

in Tunesien (Afrika).

R. I. P.

Death notice of a paratrooper killed in February 1943. The picture shows him as an aviator—he may have been an injured airman posted to a Fallschirmjäger unit or a pilot who washed out and joined the Luftwaffe ground forces.

In Profile:
Fighter aircraft

Bf 109 G-2 (W.Nr 10544) of 2.(H)/14 flown by Lt. Herbert Prior.

Fw 190 A-4 (W.Nr 0140 748) of 6./JG 2 flown by Oblt. Erich Rudorffer.

Fw 190 A-5 of 5./Schl.G.2.

Fallschirmjäger in Tunisia

While the Ramcke Brigade was desperately fighting in the El Alamein sector, new paratroop units were soon due to reach Africa. When the Allied landings in North Africa were announced Feldmarschall Kesselring ordered Hptm. Paul Sauer to assemble all the Fallschirmjäger available in the Athens area. These were detachments already awaiting departure to reinforce the Ramcke Brigade, but also soldiers on leave, convalescents discharged from hospitals, and soldiers imprisoned for disciplinary reasons. This small, diverse troop was loaded onto Ju 52s and, via Brindisi and Catania, landed on November 10 at El Aouina, Tunis. The Vichy authorities in Tunis were reluctant to accept this arrival and considered it an invasion. However, from the beginning, the detachment was warmly welcomed by the indigenous Arab population who saw the Germans, with their notably anti-colonialist worldview, as liberators.

The newcomers would rapidly take control of the two major airfields of El Aouina and La Marsa (Bizerte). When the report was submitted to Obst. Martin Harlinghausen, the new Fliegerführer Tunesien, he ordered the security perimeter to be extended to the port of Tunis, which took place on November 14.

In Germany, I., II., and II./FJR 5 (5th Parachute Regiment) were placed on immediate standby. It reached Caserta on November 10, arriving at El Aouina the next day ... during a bombing raid.

Reinforcements were now gradually reaching Tunisia, often thanks to the Me 323 transports of I./KGzbV 323. The FJR 5 was thus reinforced by pioneers commanded by the famous Maj. Rudolf Witzig who had reduced the Belgian fort of Eben Emael on May 10, 1940.

Very quickly, the Fallschirmjäger were deployed in delaying actions to counter the Allied thrust from the west, pending the arrival of the Afrika Korps full retreat from the east. They also had to keep an eye on the French units in Tunisia, considered unreliable. Throughout the duration of the Tunisian campaign, the Fallschirmjäger fought vigorously on several fronts, for some six months. But despite their tenacity, they could not prevent the fall of the "*Festung Tunesien*" or "Fortress Tunisia" in May 1943. Those who could not escape to Europe were captured.

These paratroopers engaged in combat in Tunisia snatch a bite to eat. Their losses were high.

Tactical recce Staffel 2.(H)/14 returned to Africa to support the Afrika Korps' retreat to Tunisia. The Staffel was now flying Bf 109s exclusively.

pilots of the detachment from I./JG 53 still in Benghazi gave up their serviceable Bf 109s to JG 27 and returned to Sicily in Ju 52 transports for onward deployment to Tunisia. The short-range recce Staffel 2.(H)/14, which had returned to Germany several months earlier, was sent back to Africa. According to the short history of the squadron: "Once again, in October 1942, the Staffel moved to southern Italy and settled in at Pancrazio airfield … On November 13, the first transports left for Tunis. The unit was fully equipped with Bf 109s." Indeed, 2.(H)/14 henceforth only flew single-engined aircraft. Another army-cooperation Staffel, 4.(H)/12, present in Libya, did likewise, gradually giving up its Bf 110s to III./ZG 26 where they were much needed. On November 13, the Stab./JG 27 and I./JG 27 left for Germany for rest and refit, while III./JG 27 moved to Crete to carry out patrols and escort missions. Only II./JG 27, which took over III./JG 27's aircraft, remained temporarily on African soil. On November 14, II./JG 51, which had been in Trapani since the 8th, landed at Bizerte. On November 15, after receiving a visit from the Inspector of Fighters in the West, Oberst Günther Lützow, 11./JG 2 was officially transferred to the airfield at Bizerte, Sidi Ahmed. These Bf 109 pilots, supposedly specialist high-altitude fighters, found themselves increasingly mis-employed from November 17, flying strafing sorties near Bizerte. An attempt was made to integrate 11./JG 2 into JG 53 but, at Staka Meimberg's insistence, the merger was postponed. II./JG 2 in turn moved to Africa. On November 17, the Fw 190s of II./JG 2 left France for Comiso. For several days, the pilots flew various escort missions, mainly for the benefit of the air and sea transport fleets linking Sicily to the Tunisian bridgehead. On November 24, 10 Fw 190s equipped with auxiliary tanks reached Sidi Ahmed. These aircraft, the first Focke-Wulf fighters to arrive in Africa, were considered by Kesselring as being of "very special importance" and therefore took precedence.

Meanwhile, the bombing units based in Sicily were doing what they could. On November 10, as the Eighth Army pushed west, with the Allies facing off against the French in Morocco and Algeria, LG 1 was split between ship escort duties, often to Tripoli, and attacks on the invasion fleet: permission had now been given to bomb ships anchored in the port of Algiers, which was Vichy territory. On November 11, as the Wehrmacht invaded the so-called "unoccupied zone" in France, 50 Ju 88s from LG 1, KG 54, KG 77 and III./KG 30, supported by three KG 26 He 111s, attacked the Algerian port of Bougie in two waves. On November 12, a similar number of bombers returned to Bougie. These raids thus continued but on occasion were only sporadic in nature due to the limited number of aircraft available.

Oblt. Julius "Jule" Meimberg, Staka of 11./JG 2, climbing out of his machine after a mission over Tunisia. It was mooted that 11./JG 2 was to be absorbed by JG 53 upon its arrival in theater. Meimberg did everything possible to postpone this.

On November 13, 1942, the Stab./JG 27 left Africa to return to Europe. Kommodore Edu Neumann, who had been one of the first German fighter pilots in Libya, later refused to take command any other Geschwader, regarding JG 27 as the best fighter unit in the Luftwaffe. He is seen here in conversation with Adolf Galland, Inspector of Fighters, who is on an inspection visit to the desert. Galland and Neumann both served in the same unit in the Spanish Civil War.

The Fw 190s of II./JG 2 were also dispatched to Tunisia, the first aircraft of this type to operate in Africa.

Very quickly, the Luftwaffe would fly bombing raids against Algiers. But Anglo-American forces soon deployed antiaircraft batteries assisted by searchlights. Hence this profusion of beams sweeping the Algerian night sky.

On September 3, 1942, Oblt. Martin Mossdorf leading 3./St.G. 3 was presented with the Knight's Cross by Fliegerführer Afrika, Gen. Hans Seidemann. On November 11, 1942, Mossdorf was shot down and captured in one of the last major air battles fought by the Ju 87s of St. G. 3 in the Libyan desert.

Falling Back on Tunisia

With the Allied landings, the Luftwaffe was once again split. While one part defended Tunisia, with reinforcements that would normally have been assigned to Libya, the other covered the inevitable retreat of the Afrika Korps. On November 8, British tanks reached Mersa Matruh. The Stab and the two Gruppen of JG 77, still supported by II./JG 27, struggled to slow the enemy advance, and at the cost of serious losses. In his diary, Armin Köhler wrote on November 9:

> Major Müncheberg's briefing. The Afrika Korps is on the verge of being wiped out. He quoted an order from Göring to the fighters in Africa. He's got it wrong and it is surprising to see how poorly the situation on the ground is understood. The fighter arm is somehow responsible for Rommel's retreat, so to speak. Of course we don't see it like that. If no supplies reach us, then when the last aircraft are lost we will have to fight with hand weapons alongside the Afrika Korps until the end. Müncheberg added: "We will probably never see Europe again."

While Luftwaffe fighters continued to resist fiercely in the face of the enemy's numerical superiority, the Ju 87s, present from the outset in Africa, did not give up. But on November 11, Kittyhawks intercepted a formation of about 20 Stukas near Gambut, almost everything that St. G. 3 could muster in the desert. The weak fighter escort was swept away and, for a few casualties, the Allied pilots shot down some 10 Ju 87s. Oblt. and recent recipient of the Knight's Cross Martin Mossdorf was taken captive. Wisely, the Ju 87s were evacuated to Sicily and Sardinia to allow them to refit. Ground support duties fell henceforth to the Bf 109s of SG 2.

I. and III. /JG 77 were to cover the Afrika Korps' retreat to Tunisia. The many, often bloody, aerial battles nevertheless allowed the pilots to conduct a few game hunts in the desert to improve their limited rations, as supplies had became increasingly rare. From left: the new Kommodore, Maj. Joachim Müncheberg, Hptm. Heinz Bär (Kdr I./JG 77), Oblt. Emil Omert (Staka 8./JG 77), Maj. Kurt Ubben (Kdr III./JG 77), and unidentified.

Some I./JG 77 aircraft adopted a sophisticated camouflage similar to that of Regia Aeronautica machines and referred to by the British as “sand and spinach.” Note the “top hat” badge of 2./JG 77 on the rear fuselage.

During their advance, the Eighth Army seized dozens of aircraft abandoned for lack of fuel or spare parts. This was the case at Bir el Arca for “black 6,” Lt. Heinz Lüdemann’s 8./JG 77 Gustav, damaged on November 4.

An Hs 129 of 4./SG 2 recently arrived and flying operations in the desert.

The airfields occupied by the Luftwaffe were heavily bombed as here at Castel Benito.

On November 13, Tobruk was retaken. Some Ju 88s of LG 1 operating over Algeria and Morocco returned to Heraklion and Kastelli in Crete to bomb British columns near the Halfaya Pass. On November 14, Axis forces evacuated Derna as well as the airfields of Tmimi and Martuba. That evening, LG 1 Junkers twins were engaged in a futile search for an Allied convoy between Alexandria and Tobruk while some Ju 88s, airborne from Heraklion bombed British columns near Sollom. On November 15, in the morning, I. and II./ LG 1 flew sorties over Halfaya.

The fighters on the other hand were subject to the laws of diminishing returns. On November 15, Köhker wrote: "We are with Hptm. Rödel's Gruppe. We are at cockpit readiness. At about 3 p.m. 18 four-engined aircraft attacked our aerodrome. We have no Flak or antiaircraft defenses, no lookouts or Freya." Despite this, some fighters got airborne and at least one B-24 was shot down.

Operations over Egypt continued but with less vigor. On November 16, during a reconnaissance over Port Said, a Ju 88 of 5./LG 1 was shot down by 94 Squadron Hurricanes over the Nile Delta. The Bf 110s of III./ZG 76 were active but suffered losses. On November 17, the newly arrived Henschel Hs 129s of 4./SG 2 flew their first mission over the front, claiming 12 British tanks destroyed. On November 19, Benghazi fell and the German fighters fell back.

On November 20, the *Tagjagd* in Libya was deployed as follows:

- Arco Philaenorum: Stab/JG 77 x 4 Bf 109; I./JG 77 x 18 Bf 109; III./JG 77 x 17 Bf 109.
- Nofilia/Merduma: II./JG 27 x 35 Bf 109 (the unit received aircraft from I. and III./ JG 27).

To this, we can add the seven Bf 109s of 4.(H)/12 also at Arco. Although reconnaissance pilots had not been trained as fighters, they occasionally had to face enemy aircraft. However, of these 81 Bf 109s, only 43 were flightworthy, far too few to cope with the Allied air tsunami. On December 5, the first II./JG 77 Bf 109s arrived at Zazur from Russia. II./JG 27 gave up their serviceable aircraft and then left Africa for the last time. The engagements in the air continued relentlessly as reported in his diary by the Austrian Hptm. Erwin Bacsila, attached to the Stab/JG 77:

> December 7: In the afternoon, combat with a much more numerous opponent. We have nine machines and the opponent about thirty. Our position was very bad from the beginning but we get away with it and get two kills (Major Müncheberg and myself). [Note: Bacsila's was not confirmed.]

Theodor Lindemann jumps down from his Bf 109. A personal friend of Kommodore Müncheberg's, he had, at his own request, joined the Stab/JG 77 and been appointed adjutant.

> December 8: At noon, a strafing attack by British fighter-bombers on our runway. Two Schwärme take off. We shoot down four Curtisses and lose one Bf 109. I see him dive from 2,000 meters and plunge into the sea. An American pilot bails out and also comes down in the sea. Despite our efforts, we were unable to save him … What I feared has happened. With his superiority, the opponent can "operate at will" … For tomorrow, the Geschwader has only 12 aircraft that are still serviceable. The opponent can line up 130 to 150 planes. An unequal fight! Fortunately, they have a healthy respect for our fighters.

The Luftwaffe threw every available aircraft into the fray. On the night of December 12, a III./KG 76 Ju 88 was lost near Agedabia, having probably arrived as a reinforcement from Sicily. On December 14, JG 77 was again bombed. Another tanker was torpedoed, the lack of fuel preventing combat missions from being flown. The next day, the unit evacuated to the west. Many pilots had to travel overland due to a lack of aircraft and fuel. Bacsila arrived at 2200 in Tlamed, again during a bombing raid: his column had already been attacked shortly prior to this at Sirte. There were further attacks on December 16, as the men prepared a makeshift airfield, Bacsila noting: "We spent three hours uninterrupted in our slit trenches, surprised to be still alive. These air attacks are starting to affect the men's nerves." On December 17, the unit again moved back when enemy troops were reported in the area. During the evening of the 18th, the remnants of JG 77 fell back to Tauorga. It was here that they were lucky enough to receive mail from home.

On December 18, the aerodrome at Arco came into use by the British, who could now penetrate deep into Tripolitania. On December 22, near Benghazi, a Ju 88 of II./KG 26 and an He 111 of I./KG 26 were lost. Again, these were aircraft committed from Sicily in support of LG 1, which had its work cut out. For the past 10 days, its Ju 88s had in fact escalated their night missions to Benghazi and Tobruk, where enemy ships supplying the Eighth

To slow the advance of the Eighth Army, LG 1 launched its Ju 88 bombers at night against Tobruk and Benghazi. But during these operations, the Geschwader lost two Knight's Cross recipients and the Kommodore within six days. One of the RKTs was Hptm. Erwin Sy, while Kommodore von Benda flew as part of his crew.

Army were assembled en masse. During these risky operations, the Lehrgeschwader lost its commander and two of its Knight's Cross recipients. On December 2, Hptm. Erwin Sy was reported missing, along with the Kommodore, Obstlt. Franz von Benda, during a sortie over Tobruk. On December 7, the Ju 88 flown by Oblt. Gerhard Backhaus crashed into the sea shortly after takeoff from Heraklion. On the night of December 29/30, three bombers of 4./LG 1 raided the Arco Philaenorum airfield, now in British hands. Antiaircraft defenses proved effective and a Ju 88 failed to return to Sicily.

The frantic pace of operations adversely affected many units on both sides. By late 1942, II./KG 100 and the Stab had only four full crews, while, due to reinforcements received, some 22 Heinkels were serviceable. Continuing the fight under these conditions was fast becoming impossible given the high loss rates. The KG 100 Wiking detachments in the Mediterranean soon had to be withdrawn for rest and refit.

On New Year's Day 1943, JG 77 filed the following strength return:

Stab/JG 77: 7 x Bf 109 (5) 11 pilots (6) (Bir Dufan)

I./JG 77: 25 x Bf 109 (11) 43 pilots (29) (Bir Dufan)

II./JG 77: 24 x Bf 109 (17) 23 pilots (22) (Zarzur)

III./JG 77: 30 x Bf 109 (15) 49 pilots (35) (Bir Dufan)

JG 77 fought on courageously. Although it was retreating, the Geschwader claimed 11 kills on January 13 and no less than 28 on the 14th. This was in large measure down to the unit's *Experten*: Müncheberg, Ubben, and Hackler, among others. These successes were, however, tempered by the losses suffered by I./JG 77: no fewer than three pilots. Ofw. Walter Brandt, a 36-kill veteran of I./LG 2 was shot down by Kittyhawks. He was able to bail out south of Buerat but had lost a lot of blood and ultimately had a leg amputated. He was presented with the Knight's Cross in hospital. He returned to combat flying with a false limb, but flew no further sorties with JG 77. As a Staka in JG 3 he returned a further five kills.

Hptm. Bacsila recalled the events of the 14th:

> January 14, 1943: a busy day. Already, early in the morning, the English appeared overhead. I flew four sorties and, each time, I came up against a much superior enemy numerically. I think I returned two kills, but I could not see where they

On January 14, a British fighter pilot was shot down near Bir Dufan airfield occupied by JG 77. The pilot was greeted graciously by his German counterparts. From left: Ofw. Robert Helmer (KIA February 26, 1943), Oblt. Georg Seckel, the RAF pilot, Uffz. Max Denhardt (POW on March 24, 1943), unidentified, and Lt. Heinz Lüdemann (KIA on March 10, 1943).

> came down because I attacked Kittyhawks from the rear on both occasions. It is true that a large number of wrecks have been identified, but the victors could not be ascertained. Maybe mine were among these? In any case, it was a great event. When, at noon, we came back on our last drops of fuel we saw 18 English bombers pounding our airfield with impunity in the distance. In the end we had to land between the bomb craters; it was no picnic. But the Geschwader shot down 28 Englishmen that day.

On January 19, II./JG 77 left Libya and flew to the Tunisian aerodrome of Medenine. By around January 20, the front had almost reached Tripoli. I./JG 77 spent the same day at Ben Gardane. III./JG 77 followed suit and reached Matmata. Finally, on January 22, the Stab/JG 77, the last element of the Geschwader still in Libya, left for Zuara. JG 77 had thus departed Libya for good and relocated near the border. Its fighters were now also able to operate eastward against the Eighth Army, but they also now found themselves in the area covered by USAAF aircraft based in Algeria and would also come up against P-38s, B-17s, B-24s, and B-25s. Although kills were rarer for JG 77 at that time, the *Abschüsse* returned by Hptm. Bär were of note: six P-40s and two P-38s between January 21 and 27.

Despite the losses, despite the continuous harassment by the ubiquitous and superior Allied air forces, and overcoming supply problems of all kinds, JG 77 fulfilled a difficult task. After El Alamein, everyone believed that the Geschwader would be destroyed in the desert, but the unit's pilots successfully managed to cover the retreat of the Panzerarmee Afrika to the Tunisian border. But, for JG 77, the fighting was far from over.

In the January 14 dogfight Ofw. Walter Brandt was shot down. The 36-kill ace was seriously injured and had a leg amputated. He received the Knight's Cross while in hospital and ended the war with JG 3.

Tunisia

While JG 77 attempted to slow the Eighth Army's advance to the east, the Axis were organizing their defenses in Tunisia. The rapid German reaction would have come as a surprise to the Allied high command, who believed it could take control of the country fairly quickly. With only limited resources to hand, the Luftwaffe established a Fliegerkorps Tunis, with General Martin Harlinghausen designated as Fliegerführer Tunesien.

In addition to the Ju 52 and Me 323 transports, the huge BV 222 seaplanes of LTS (See) 222 were widely used to ferry men and equipment to Tunis. The Lufttransportführer Mittelmeer, Generalmajor Ulrich Buchholz, hastily formed two transport squadrons, S (Sicily) and N (Naples), to speed up resupply shipments. But only experienced crews could land at Gabès and Sfax, these aerodromes having very basic facilities. The Ju 52s flew day and night in loose formation for fear of prowling British nightfighters. As Gundelach observed: "The Tunis–Tripoli air supply route began with improvisation and right up to the end was constantly improvised. But these very costly sorties to North Africa could not change the situation."

II./JG 53 was initially attached to Bizerte, while III./JG 53 was assigned to the defense of the Tunis region from El Aouina. In fact, during all this time and until the end of 1942, the "Pik As" would be split between Bizerte, Mateur, and El Aouina; while also using satellite fields like Djedeida, the Geschwader was mainly concentrated at Bizerte.

Reinforcements arrived from all parts, often haphazardly. Thus, II./St. G. 3, which had evacuated Libya due to its losses, left Sardinia where it had withdrawn, to settle in Djedeida near Tunis. On November 18, a handful of their Stukas supported a German ground unit at Medjed-el-Bab, which made it possible to capture the area. In his memoirs, Winston Churchill acknowledged the quality and bluff of this attack, the success of which had depended on just a few aircraft.

From Tunis-El Aouina Ju 52 and Me 323 transports flew in relays, bringing reinforcements into the "*Festung Tunesien.*"

Sent urgently to Africa with Oblt. Julius Meimberg's 11./JG 2, Ofw. Günther Seeger was soon to claim fresh kills.

On November 26, a remarkable battle added to the local confusion. Two days earlier, the US 1st Armored Division had landed in Tunisia and, on the 26th, 17 M-3 tanks launched an assault over the plain of Djedeida against the airfield, in the manner of a cavalry charge. The assault took the Germans by surprise. The Bf 109s of JG 53 on the field were scrambled to strafe the attackers but some 15 Ju 87s of II./St. G. 3 were reportedly destroyed as well as a number of hangars. The fighters claimed some of the tanks wrecked, but the Americans would only acknowledge two destroyed. The area would be taken and then lost again in subsequent fighting. Despite these losses, the crews of the surviving Ju 87s fought on, sinking the cruiser HMS *Ithuriel* and "terrorizing" the GIs. Complaints quickly arrived at General George Patton's HQ asking why no action was being taken against the "repeated attacks by the supposedly obsolete German Stukas."

The most significant losses in German aircraft were caused by airfield raids. However, the aces once again demonstrated their proficiency. On November 27, Ofw. Günther Seeger of 11./JG 2 claimed his first "African" kill, and his 25th in total: a P-38 shot down over the sea. On November 29, the first Hs 129 twin-engined assault aircraft of 5. /Sch. G. 1, shortly to be renamed 8.(Pz) Schl.G.2), as well as the Fw 190s of 5. /SG 1 that had previously fought on the Eastern Front, arrived at El Aouina. On November 30, III./ZG 2 (which arrived in October in Sidi Ahmed) was redesignated III./SKG 10, the Gruppe still equipped with the Fw 190.

Oblt. and Knight's Cross recipient Hans Röhrig posing with his 9./JG 53.

In early 1943 the propaganda magazine *Signal* published this photo of 4./JG 51 ace, Lt. and Knight's Cross recipient, Anton Hafner, seen with a P-38 pilot he has just shot down. "Toni" Hafner was credited with seven Lightnings in Tunisia before being shot down and seriously wounded himself on January 14, 1943 over Pont-du-Fahs. However, he returned to his unit several months later.

December 1942

December 1 saw the beginning of a major German counteroffensive in Tunisia with the Luftwaffe considerably augmenting its effort. On December 2, as events ran their course, the Kommandeur of III./ZG 2, Hptm. Wilhelm Hachfeld, taking off from Sidi Ahmed, collided with an Fw 190 A-3 of II./JG 2. Hachfeld's aircraft nosed over and caught fire and the pilot died in the resulting conflagration. "Bomben-Willi" Hachfeld had been flying since the beginning of the war and with 11 kills had been a fighter ace with JG 51 in Russia, prior to becoming a Jabo specialist. He had been awarded the Knight's Cross just two months previously.

On December 3, B-17s bombed El Aouina, surprising 11./JG 26 and killing half its pilot complement: six. The Staffel was then disbanded and the surviving personnel distributed in II./JG 51. The *Tagjäger* occasionally enjoyed success: December 4 was notable for a full-scale massacre of Bisley transports. A formation of 12 of these aircraft from 614 Squadron and 18 Squadron operating unescorted ran into I. and II./JG 53, and 11. /JG 2, and all 12 Bisleys were shot down in quick time. December 5 would also

Unser lieber Sohn und Bruder

HERBERT MOSER

Leutnant in einer Kampfgruppe z. b. V.

starb am 18. Dezember 1942

23 Jahre alt

in Nordafrika den Fliegertod

Er hat sein Leben für uns zum Opfer gebracht und er hat gewonnen, was auch wir gewinnen müssen, um es dauernd zu besitzen – den Frieden.

Vater unser — Ave Maria

Friedrich Pustet, Regensburg

One of the many Luftwaffe transport crews killed, Lt. Moser was a Ju 52 pilot with KGzbV S 11, based in Brindisi, a unit hastily formed to supply Tunisia. He died at El Aouina on December 18 after his plane hit an obstacle.

On December 30, Lt. Hubert Greim (11./JG 2) was shot down and captured. He was the only son of General von Greim, a Great War ace and senior Luftwaffe officer. As his father's title was not transferable, Hubert could not prefix his surname with "von."

be an equally exhausting day as a result of almost constant bombing raids, this time American. No fewer than 11 P-38s were officially lost that day over Sidi Ahmed, with six claimed by the "Pik As." However, the onset of particularly bad weather would hamper air operations.

On December 26, when the USAAF once again attacked the port of Bizerte, its aircraft clashed with JG 53 and II./JG 2, with one bomber and two P-38s shot down. However, a steady stream of losses continued to weaken the Luftwaffe in Tunisia. On December 30, Lt. Hubert Greim, regular wingman for the Kapitän of 11./JG 2, was shot down and taken captive. According to his own account:

> We were supposed to attack the British airfield at Souk el Arba. Over the target, we were attacked by enemy fighters and my Gustav was hit by gunfire. So I was forced to put it down near Tabarka. I landed gear up without too much difficulty and was captured by Spahis [French-Algerian troops]. I was sent to Constantine where it was soon discovered that I was the son of the famous Ritter von Greim. After a short interrogation, I was sent to Bône and then to Gibraltar. After a stint in England, I finished the war in captivity in the USA and did not return from Trinidad until March 1946.

"Toni" Hafner's Bf 109 alongside the runway in El Aouina.

German airborne operations

On December 20, at his headquarters in Frascati, Feldmarschall Albert Kesselring hosted Hptm. Gerhard Schacht, an experienced parachute officer attached to the Ramcke Brigade, entrusting him with six Ju 52s of IV./KGzbV 1 with crews skilled in blind flying, 12 DFS 230 gliders of 2. (DFS)/VK (S) 2 as well as three He 111s. Flying in from Castelvetrano on December 26, 1942, this small force arrived at Bizerte. There, it was learned that a mission would take place the next day with the support of Brandenburger commandos. Two groups were established: three DFS 230s were scheduled to drop off the Brandenburgers at Sidi Bou Baker, and three other DFS 230s would do likewise near a bridge northeast of Kasserine. These bridges could not be attacked by Ju 87s. Five gliders were lost during this operation, but most of the men were able to return on foot, often with the help of the local population. One of the bridges was reportedly destroyed. According to two British interrogation reports, another such operation took place on the night of December 29/30, to destroy a rail bridge near St Arnaud. This series of sabotage missions was conducted with glider pilots attached to combat units, St.G. 3 and JG 53. This suggests, taking into account the pilots and gliders subsequently flown on December 26, that this type of air sabotage operation was repeated, probably exceeding 10 and perhaps even as many as 20 such raids by the end of 1942. Unfortunately, there is no record of all of them.

During December 1942 Luftwaffe strength in Tunisia comprised:

Stab/JG 53	Bf 109 G (Bizerte)
I./JG 53	Bf 109 G (Mateur)
III./JG 53	Bf 109 G (Mateur)
5 /JG 53	Bf 109 G (Gabès)
II./JG 51	Bf 109 G (La Sebala)
III./SKG 10	Fw 190 (Sidi Ahmed)
5./SG 1	Fw 190 (El Aouina)
8./SG 2	Hs 129 B (El Aouina)
II./St.G. 3	Ju 87 D (La Sebala)
2.(H)/14	Bf 109 F4/R3 (El Aouina)

January 1943

During the course of the month, German fighter units operating in Tunisia would counter both enemy fighters and bombers attacking ports, airfields, and defensive positions in the "Fortress." Luftwaffe bombers

A "Tommy" inspecting the wreck of a DFS 230 glider which may have belonged to 2./VK (S) 2, seen here abandoned in Tunisia.

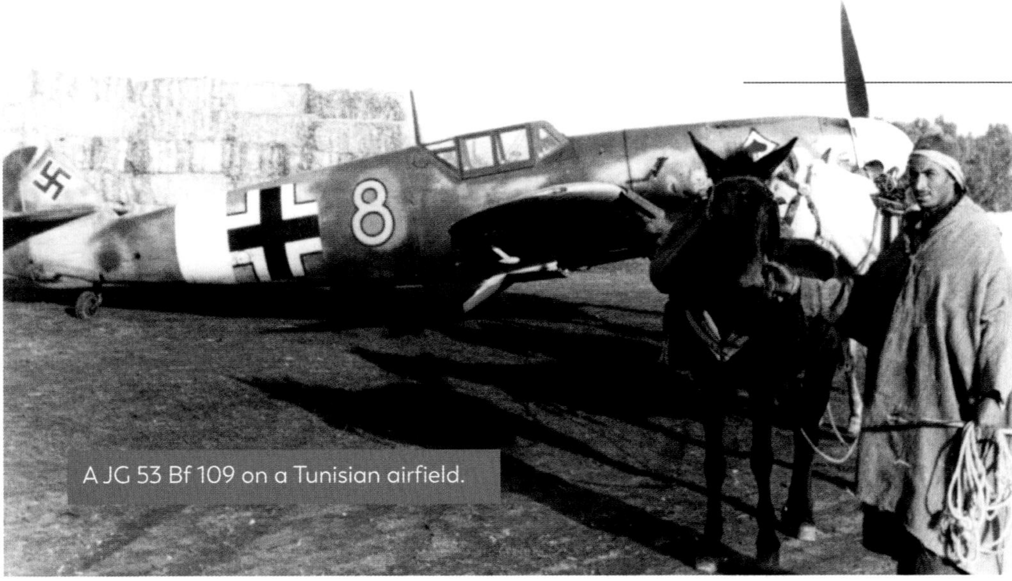

A JG 53 Bf 109 on a Tunisian airfield.

Zum stillen Gedenken
an die gefallenen Flieger
Zwillingsbrüder

Theo Niemand
Feldwebel und Bordmechaniker

Heinz Niemand
Feldwebel und Bordmechaniker

in einem Transportgeschwader,
ausgezeichnet mit Frontflugspangen und Kriegsverdienstkreuzen

Die lieben Verstorbenen wurden am 14. April 1918 zu Menden (Krs. Iserlohn) geboren und starben auf einem gemeinsamen Feindflug über dem Mittelmeer am 11. Januar 1943 den Fliegertod. In treuer Pflichterfüllung gaben sie ihr junges Leben für die geliebte Heimat. Mit großer Liebe und Sorge hingen sie bis zu ihrem Heldentode an ihren Eltern, Geschwistern und allen, die ihnen in ihrem Leben nahe standen.

Jetzt ruhen sie fern der lieben Heimat, doch ewig nahe unserm Herzen.

On January 11, 1943, an Me 323 of KGzbV 323 was shot down by P-38s off Bizerte. Among the crew killed were the two flight engineers: twins Theo and Heinz Niemand died together when their machine plunged into the sea.

A shot-down Bf 109 of II./JG 51 is examined by its victors.

Zum Andenken
an meinen lieben Gatten und Vati,
unseren unvergeßlichen Sohn und
Bruder

Oberfeldwebel Fritz Roth
Flugzeugführer
in einer Transportstaffel

Inhaber des E. K. I. und 2. Klasse,
der Frontflugspange in Silber und
Gold sowie verschiedener anderer
Militärauszeichnungen
geboren am 31. Juli 1912 in
Schwimmbach
gefallen am 22. Januar 1943
bei einem Bombenangriff in Tunis

Aus dem Brief seines Staffelführers:
„Ihr Mann war einer meiner besten Flugzeugführer, der sich durch seine nie ermüdende Einsatzfreudigkeit, seinem Schneid und Tapferkeit besonders bewährt hat.“

Ofw. Fritz Roth was a decorated KGzbV 800 Ju 52 pilot who was killed on January 22 during a raid on El Aouina.

based in Sicily and Crete returned to combat after having partially licked their wounds from the fighting over El Alamein. LG 1 operated mainly in the rear of the Eighth Army or against shipping.

On January 16, during an attack on a maritime convoy off Tobruk, two Ju 88s of 5./LG 1 that had taken off from Heraklion were shot down by Beaufighters of 98 Squadron. On the night of January 17/18, eight Ju 88s of II./LG 1 bombed troop concentrations near Benghazi. On the return to Heraklion, two aircraft collided in mid-air. On January 21/22, the Ju 88s returned to Benghazi harbor. Cloud cover was so dense that only one aircraft could find the target and drop its bombs, taking some antiaircraft strikes in the process. British nightfighters reportedly intercepted two Ju 88s but none was able to maneuver into a firing position.

On January 23, flying from Catania, LG 1 participated in a reinforced assault on the port of Bône with mines and bombs. Aircraft from KGs 30, 54, 66, and 76 were also launched. That evening, Ju 88s were airborne to attack positions at Souk el Arba. On January 24, LG 1 Ju 88s, in concert with KG 54, escorted two large cargo ships en route to Bizerte. II./KG 100

Seen through the gun camera of an Allied fighter, this was the fate of many Ju 52s strafed on their airfields in Tunisia. The "N" indicates that the aircraft was from the Naples-based transport unit. The arrow at bottom right shows a crew member lying on the ground.

Luftflotte 2 strength return, January 31, 1943

			II. Fl. Korps		X. Fl.Korps
Units	**Fl.F. Afrika**	**Fl.F Tunis**	**Sicily**	**Sardinia**	**Greece/Crete**
Tactical Reconnaissance	3 (2)	9 (6)			
Strategic Reconnaissance	5 (2)		27 (12)		
Fighters	79 (48)	89 (48)		40 (24)	11 (6)
Zerstörer			49 (24)		
Nightfighters			15 (10)		
Bombers			149 (87)	69 (37)	95 (81)
Fast Bombers		21 (8)			
Dive bombers	21 (14)	28 (22)			
Ground attack	15 (7)	7 (5)			
Seaplanes				21 (12)	
Transporters (Mediterranean)	172 (145)				

Fighters operating as close as possible to the front were based mainly in Tunisia.

The Bf 110s tasked with escort missions and too vulnerable in Africa were based in Sicily.

Similarly, for bombers, those present in Greece/Crete attacked Allied convoys and enemy movements in Libya.

The fast bombers comprised the Fw 190s of III./SKG 10 while the complement of ground support aircraft was made up of the Fw 190s of 5./SG 1 as well as the Hs 129s of 8./SG 2.

was supposed to have been withdrawn from operations at the end of 1942, but the by-now exhausted crews continued to fly missions, including one on the night of January 8/9, against Benghazi. One of the Heinkels failed to return, another reverse for an already tested unit.

On January 31, 12 P-38s of the 82nd Fighter Group escorting six B-26s off the Tunisian coast in search of enemy shipping, attacked two He 111s spotted at a higher altitude, probably from II./KG 100. Two Bf 110s of 8./ZG 26 assigned as escorts drew off the P-38s but were both shot down. When encountered during sweeps mounted by Allied fighters, Luftwaffe transport aircraft were easily picked off. On January 11, eight P-38s of the 49th Fighter Squadron escorting bombers north of Bizerte ran across a mixed formation of Ju 52s and Me 323 transports. Two Ju 52s were claimed while Lt. Moore reported that he shot down a six-engined aircraft. Nine airmen and 16 passengers aboard this *Gigant* were killed. Four days later, on the 15th, in a similar scenario, eight P-38s of the 48th FS also ran into some Luftwaffe transports. Lt. Shipman was credited with one "six-engined" aircraft damaged. In actual fact, Me 323 DT+IK crashed near Bizerte with 12 on board.

A III./JG 77 machine forced to make an emergency landing at Matmata.

As the Luftwaffe could no longer provide sufficient escorts, ships shuttling between Tunisia and Sicily could easily be attacked at low altitude, such as this Italian tanker targeted by an American bomber.

February 1943

At the start of the month, the Bf 110s of III./ZG 26 escorting transport formations had their work cut out. Approaching the Tunisian coast, they were being continuously intercepted by Allied fighters well informed as they were by Ultra. On February 2, 16 P-38s of the 96th Bomb Group escorting B-26s in a sea sweep intercepted an Axis air convoy. Multiple kills were claimed by the American pilots. A single P-38 might have been lost, victim of the escort. On February 3, it was again during a Marauder escort that 12 P-38s of the 96th Fighter Squadron ran into four Bf 110s protecting two tankers returning empty from Bizerte to Italy. Two Bf 110 F-2s were shot down as well as one Lightning. On the same day, a major clash took place between 5./JG 53 and a formation of B-26s. These medium bombers were appearing in increasing numbers on the JG 53 "scoreboard," proof of the growing commitment of the USAAF to Tunisia. Initial fighter-versus-fighter contests over the desert had been superceded by a war that could only be described as a "battle of matériel." Numerical superiority in the air was the preserve of the Allies.

On February 4, remnants of the Panzerarmee Afrika crossed the Tunisian border from the east and deployed in defensive positions along the Mareth Line. Poor weather conditions in North Africa—but also problems with fuel resupply and aircraft maintenance—explained the slowdown in air operations on the German side, not to mention the increasing fatigue of airmen and ground crews.

The Fw 190s of II./JG 2 appear to have been active during February given the large number of kills claimed. They flew "free hunts" but also escorted the Ju 87s of II./St. G. 3, the Fw 190s of III./SKG 10, and the Hs 129s of 8. /SG 2.

On February 14, in the east of the country, JG 77 supported the counterattack launched by General Jürgen von Arnim toward Kasserine and Tebessa against the American First Army. This operation was initially a success, driving an important wedge between the Allied lines. The next day, Generalfeldmarschall Erwin Rommel, in the southern sector of the Axis forces, executed the same maneuver and took Gafsa. On February 15, aircraft from 8./JG 77 took off from Matmata to strafe an airfield

On February 13, a Bf 109 F-4 of I./SG 2 was shot down by antiaircraft fire near Gafsa. The pilot, Uffz. Willi Reuter, was captured but was able to escape after eight days. With the help of the local populace, he managed to return to his unit, wearing a djellaba. His adventure earned him the nickname "Muli" (donkey).

To relieve congestion at regularly bombed airfields, the Hs 129s of 8./SG 2 would on occasion use roads to take off.

at Thelepte. The Germans overran Kasserine on February 18; however, they were unable to take advantage of their breakthrough due to inadequate supply lines. On the 20th, Axis forces withdrew to the Mareth Line. On the 23rd, the Axis ground forces were placed under Rommel's sole command. On February 26, the battle ended with the Allies retaking Kasserine. The Allies suffered 10,000 casualties and the Germans two thousand.

LG 1 temporarily restructured its Ju 88 operations. I./LG 1 continued its missions to Libya from Eleusis and Heraklion while elements of II./LG 1 deployed to Catania to be closer to Tunisia.

On February 7, four Ju 88s launched an attack on the port of Tripoli. The next day, two further raids took place over Tripoli, the first supported by He 111s of II./KG 100. During the second, 145 Squadron shot down a Ju 88.

The night of February 17/18 saw a major operation: an attack on the port of Benghazi with 18 I./LG 1 aircraft supported by four II./KG 100 He 111s. Despite the low altitude adopted for more accurate bombing—1,200 meters—and powerful antiaircraft defenses guided by searchlights, the operation took place without incident. No nightfighters were seen. On the night of February 20/21, LG 1 raided the port of Tobruk with 19 Ju 88s. The operation was a success but, on the way home a 46 Squadron Beaufighter shot down a bomber.

Elsewhere, in view of its losses, II./KG 100 drew reinforcements from whereever it could: its training unit or from aircraft and crews transferred in from KG 53. Despite their reverses and the numerical superiority of their adversaries, the encircled fighter units in Tunisia continued to give battle; for example, on February 26, JG 77 flew several sorties over the Medenine sector, targeting British troops. I./JG 77 claimed 11 P-40s (five credited to Hptm. Bär alone, who now tallied 162 kills), 10 to II./JG 77 and five to III./JG 77. But III./JG 77 lost one 1940 veteran pilot, while one of his Staka was seriously wounded and another pilot was captured.

At Kairouan, General Martin Harlinghausen (second from left), the Fliegerführer Tunesien, is seen in discussion with the Kommodore of JG 53, Obstlt. Günther Frhr. von Maltzahn. Between them in the background is Hptm. Fritz Schröter, Kommandeur of III./SKG 10.

In Profile:
Messerschmitt 110 Fighters

Bf 110 D-1/U-1 of I./NGJ 3.

Bf 110 D-3 of 7./ZG 26.

Luftwaffe transport operations, February 1943

	I./KGzbV 323	Ju 52 units	Total
Missions flown	104	1,303	1,407
Kilometers flown	114, 410	1,525,505	1,637,915
Flights into North Africa			
Munitions (to) transported:	54,176	341,567	395,743
Fuel (lit.) transported:	322,800	292,940	615,740
Aircraft spares/equipment:	162,119	221,044	383,163
Equipment (diverse):	–	650,342	650,342
Materiel for the Heer:	651,434	419,836	1,071,270
Personnel:	563	5,151	5,714
Return flights			
Wounded evacuated:	82	283	365
Personnel:	1,068	8,855	9,923
Matériel:	394,469	141,821	536,290
Fuel burnt:	960,669	3,498,712	4,459,381

This table gives an overview of the effort made by the Transportgeschwader in shipping men and equipment to Tunisia. Me 323s carried vehicles first and foremost, with soldiers embarking mainly on the three-engined Ju 52s.

A Ju 88 shot down by antiaircraft fire over Tunisia.

An Fw 190 at Tindja to reinforce II./JG 2, still wearing its factory codes. The Gruppe departed Tunisia in mid-March.

Tunisian airfields came under almost continuous bombardment.

Mechanic Reinhold Omert, younger brother of Oblt. Emil Omert, Staka 8./JG 77, in front of Fw 190 A-5/U3 Trop "white H" from 5./SG 1. Having located his brother in Tunisia, Staka Omert had him transferred to his own unit and evacuated him to Sicily.

A III./SKG 10 Fw 190 being serviced. This unit would also leave Tunisia at the end of March but continued operations from Sicily.

March 1943

For the Luftwaffe single-engined fighters, March 1943 would consist of a series of fierce clashes against well-escorted bombers and opposing fighters operating in large formations. Nervousness was such that, on March 3, pilots of JG 53 accidentally shot down a 6./JG 2 Fw 190. The pilot killed was one of the last Battle of Britain veterans in the unit. In mid-March, II./JG 2 left Africa and gave up its Fw 190s to III./SKG 10 at Tindja. II./JG 2, despite many claims, enjoyed little success in Tunisian skies, probably due to difficulties in keeping its aircraft serviceable.

Another major blow struck the *Tagjagd* on March 23. Lt. Gerhard Strasen, attached to the Stab./JG 77 recalled:

> On the morning of the 23rd, I took off with Major Müncheberg. Performing a reconnaissance over the front, we saw a small formation of Spitfires below us. Although there were only two of us, we attacked them. Fighting against enemies in greater numbers had become a regular occurence. With Müncheberg in the lead, we dived in. The Kommodore eased into a firing position behind the last Spitfire and gave it a burst of fire. It exploded a brief moment later. Because of Müncheberg's high speed he was unable to avoid the debris of his victim, some of it striking his Bf 109, which immediately became uncontrollable. Müncheberg crashed without being able to jump clear.

The Kommodore was buried a few days later in the cemetery at El-Aouina in Tunis. The Luftwaffe thus lost one of its most notable fighter leaders. Holder of the Knight's Cross with Swords for his 135 kills on all fronts, had earned the respect of his men as well as his superiors; in memory of its first leader to fall in combat the Geschwader adopted his personal badge, the red heart, displayed in 1941 in Sicily on his 7./JG 26 Emil. If JG 53 was nicknamed "Pik As," JG 77 would become the Jagdgeschwader "*Herz As*": the Ace of Hearts.

The Ju 88 bombers of LG 1 were also very busy during the month as confirmed by their sorties: on March 8, during a support mission just in advance of the German lines in Tunisia, a Ju 88 was shot down near Gabès by a nightfighter. On March 15, II./LG 1 successfully bombed a concentration of vehicles on

On March 23, Kommodore Müncheberg was killed. He was buried in a lavish ceremony in El Aouina. His death was felt as keenly as that of JG 27 ace, Hans-Joachim Marseille.

With the departure of many air defense units, the protection of German troops in the Tunisian redoubt fell largely to the Flak. This Vierling is seen in front of the famous Roman amphitheater of El Djem.

the Medenine–Ben Fardac road. On March 16, LG 1 returned to Tunisia to attack troop concentrations near Medenine. From 19 March 19, LG 1, KG 30, KG 54, KG 76, and KG 77 employed every serviceable aircraft—around 50 machines—to attack troop concentrations in the Mareth Line sector and on roads leading to Ksar Rhilane.

The situation of the encircled army became so critical that the Ju 88s were called on to temporarily abandon their role as escorts and bombers, to become transports. I./LG 1 was ordered to Grottaglie (Apulia) at the end of March where its Ju 88s were "converted" into fuel transport aircraft. The fuel tanks were filled to the brim (3,600 liters), with the twin-engined aircraft carrying a 900-liter container under each wing. On arrival at Tunis-El Aouina, the precious liquid was pumped into drums, leaving just enough fuel for the Ju 88s to return to Italy. It goes without saying that such loads rendered the aircraft difficult to maneuver, while the slightest fighter attack threatened to ignite the load and obliterate the aircraft. II./KG 100 continued its attacks with a handful of aircraft. On March 11, it lost an He 111 over Tripoli.

As for the Ju 52s, they continued to suffer, losing several of their own in attacks by Allied fighters. Despite this, activity remained strong. According to Gundelach:

> from February 23 to March 28, some 3,800 Ju 52 and 160 Me 323 transports landed in Tunis and Bizerte and another 100 Ju 52s touched down in Sfax. Italian G.12 and S.82 transport aircraft brought about 20,843 soldiers and 1,720 tons of equipment to Tunisia in 1,306 operations from February 14 to March 31, 1943.

At the end of March, the Fw 190s of III./SKG 10 likely departed Gabes, conducting operations in Tunisia from Sicily. March 1943 was an expensive month for I./KGzbV 323, which lost five aircraft—two in Italy. On March 10, while several Me 323s were present in Tunis, bombers attacked El Aouina, destroying DT+IE and SG+RE on the runway. On March 26, RF+XE crashed on takeoff from El Aouina, killing three and injuring seven. In late March, Adolf Galland traveled to Tunis via Sicily as a passenger in a III./ZG 26 Bf 110. He could but note the terrible state of the Luftwaffe in the "*Festung Tunesien*."

In late March, General Adolf Galland arrived in Sicily to take stock of the deteriorating situation. From there he made a flying visit to Tunis as a passenger in a III./ZG 26 Bf 110.

On April 7, Bf 109 G-2 "black 6" from 2.(H)/14 was shot down by antiaircraft fire and its pilot, Lt. Herbert Prior, was captured. Note the new Staffel emblem.

April 1943: Death Throes of the German Expeditionary Force

This month marked the beginning of the end for the German expeditionary force that had arrived in Africa two years earlier.

With no let up in the pressure, II./LG 1 bombed American troop concentrations in El Guettar during the night of April 1/2. The Ju 88s of I./LG 1 which had landed in Tunis-El Aouina on March 31 with their fuel loads, carried out a new shuttle that day after refueling at Catania. The II./LG 1 aircraft remaining in Catania were to carry out nightly support operations .

But, on April 5, the Allied command launched Operation *Flax*, a major air and maritime offensive aimed at cutting German links between Tunisia and Europe. During the morning, a major clash saw some 20 Lightnings of the 96th FS attack 30 Ju 52s protected by Bf 109 and 110 escorts near the Tunisian coast. Dogfights erupted across the sky but, while the 96th occupied the escort, 26 P-38s of the 1st FS concentrated on the three-engined aircraft. Fourteen Ju 52s were reportedly shot down as were at least two Bf 110s and one Bf 109 of JG 27. Six P-38s were lost. In a bombing raid on Sicily, another 10 Ju 52s were destroyed on the ground and 65 damaged.

Flax was soon to bear fruit and, on April 7, the by-now all-encompassing Allied superiority, whether on the ground or in the air, bought home to the OKW the realization that Tunisia would soon be lost. Hitler then, predictably, ordered a stand "to the last cartridge," with air units being reinforced to provide more effective support to ground troops. Offensive action was not long in coming and, the following night, LG 1 aircraft were dispatched in two-ship Rotte formations to

Zum steten Gedenken im Gebete
an den Uffz.
Philipp Kummert
Flugzeugführer von Furth i. Wald
welcher am 10. 4. 1943 im Alter von 22 Jahren in Mittel-Tunesien abstürzte.

Die Pflicht rief mich zum Krieg hinaus
Mit Gott ging ich vom Elternhaus,
Ich dachte euer fort und fort,
Wenn ich auch weilt am fremden Ort,
Und freute mich auf's Wiedersehen,
Wenn Krieg und Sturm zu Ende gehen.
Doch anders hats der Herr gewollt,
Und hat von hier mich abgeholt,
Weiß nichts von Krieg und Erdenleid
Und bin von jeder Sorg befreit:
Drum meine Lieben, denkt stets daran
Was Gott tut, das ist wohlgetan."

On April 10, 1943, Uffz. Kummert was probably one of the last pilots of III./SKG 10 to be killed in action in Tunisia.

Although flying at wavetop height, the Me 323s of TG 5 could not avoid the carnage of April 22.

various Tunisian hotspots. JG 77 personnel could well recall the prophetic words of their late fallen Kommodore Müncheberg: "We will probably never see Europe again."

On April 11, P-38s of the 95th FS patroling between Cap Bon and Marsala intercepted a formation of 20 Ju 52s escorted by four Bf 110s, four Ju 88s, and seven Bf 109s. Eighteen Ju 52s were reportedly shot down as well as the two *Zerstörer* of 7./ZG 26. Three P-38s were also lost.

April 18 saw the so-called "Palm Sunday Massacre." With intelligence provided by Ultra, the fighters of the 64th, 65th, 66th, and 314th Fighter Squadrons cut to pieces a large formation of 65 Ju 52s escorted by 16 single-engined fighters and five Bf 110s. Twenty-four Ju 52 transports came down in the sea while a further 35 were able to make emergency landings on dry land. In addition to almost 60 three-engined transports, the loss of at least nine Bf 109s and one Bf 110 was also of note. This carnage cost just six US fighters.

April 19 saw the departure of II./JG 51 which, prior to departing for Sicily, gave up their Bf 109 G-4s to JG 77 while taking back its G-2s. Similarly, the Bf 109 Friedrichs of I./SG 2 evacuated Africa. JG 77 and 53 were the last remaining single-engined fighter units to defend the Tunisian redoubt.

On April 22, KGzbV 323, recently redesignated TG 5, flew one of its most important supply missions in Tunisia. Warned by Ultra, Kittyhawks and Spitfires intercepted the formation of Me 323 six-engined transports near the island of Zembta. Six of the I./TG 5 behemoths and eight further TG 5 machines loaded with fuel were shot down. What was to be dubbed the "Cap Bon Massacre" resulted in the death of 126 German airmen and passengers, with 19 personnel being saved, almost miraculously. Among the missing were the commander of TG 5 and two Staffelkapitäne. Despite this terrible blood-letting, a *Kampfgruppe* was formed with those Me 323s still serviceable and flights to Tunisia would continue almost until the end. Elsewhere, II./KG 100, reduced to a handful of aircraft, was returned to the Reich to be reconstituted, while LG 1 continued its support missions to a pocket of Italian-German resistance that was shrinking ever further.

On the night of April 12/13, a bombing raid on Bône harbor was scheduled with KG 77 but none of the seven LG 1 Ju 88s reached the target. On the night of April 16/17, X. Fliegerkorps dispatched six LG 1 aircraft to bomb troop concentrations

Despite heavy losses, Ju 52s continued to supply the Tunisian pocket almost until the end.

Loaded with fuel drums, Ju 52 and Me 323 transports were easy prey.

in the Medjed-el-Bab–Toukabeur sector. Despite some impressive antiaircraft fire, the mission was successfully completed. The following night, six Ju 88s raided the airfield at Souk el Arba in Tunisia, once again facing heavy antiaircraft fire that failed to hit any attackers. On the night of April 19/20, flying in two waves, 18 bombers drawn from LG 1, KG 54, KG 76, and KG 77 bombed El Djem airfield that had recently fallen to the enemy. El Djem was again attacked by three LG 1 Ju 88s on the night of April 20/21. On the night of April 23/24, 21 LG 1 bombers based in Sicily bombed tanks and columns in Medjed-el-Bab. A second attack on the same objective was carried out shortly afterward, this time by 30 Ju 88s.

The following night, Ju 88s airborne from from Italy bombed targets in Tunisia. On April 25 and 26, fresh attacks were reported in the Medjed-el-Bab area. On the night of April 26/27, 17 LG 1, KG 54, and KG 77 bombers provided support to ground troops in Tunisia. The participation of the Lehrgeschwader was limited to just three machines. During the evening of April 27, LG 1 was able to assemble eight crews to bomb ships anchored in Philippeville harbor. However, the target was obscured by cloud and the bombing was carried out haphazardly.

May 1943: Dénouement

The Axis army in Tunisia was in its death throes. But LG 1 continued operations despite the difficulties. On May 2, 17 I./LG 1 Ju 88s attacked a convoy off Benghazi, with the support of a dozen torpedo bombers from KG 26. However, the weather deteriorated, forcing the crews to abort the mission.

JG 77 received the evacuation order on May 7, and in small groups its Bf 109s flew out to Sicily. But, since the Ju 52s could no longer fly shuttles because of enemy air superiority, the Bf 109s took on ad hoc transport duties: the armor plate protecting the pilot's head was removed and the aircraft was made as light as possible so that two, three, and sometimes even four ground crew personnel could cram into the fighter's narrow fuselage.

Three 4./JG 77 survivors seen on their return to Sicily. Fw. Wilhelm Reinert (left) flew Bäumel's Bf 109 with its "owner" and a mechanic crammed into the fuselage, and shot down a Martlet during the transfer. Reinert was subsequently awarded the Knight's Cross.

Lt. Karl Ritter and his superior, Maj. Franz Götz, III./JG 53 Kommandeur, at Korbous airfield shortly before leaving Tunisia for good.

After the capitulation of Axis troops, the victorious Allies came across large numbers of wrecked aircraft at El Aouina, such as this Ju 52 ...

... and these 8./SG 2 Hs 129s.

This Fw 190, probably from III./SKG 10, appears to be in good condition ...

On May 8, a Bf 109 of the Stab./JG 77, attempting to get airborne for Europe, crashed on takeoff from Korbous. Carrying the technical officer and the Stab secretariat, the machine was dangerously overloaded. Also on board was Oblt. Helmut Meckel, a competent pilot who had flown since the beginning of the war with JG 3 and had been awarded the Knight's Cross. The three victims were quickly buried at the side of the runway. Oblt. Zeno Bäumel (4./JG 77) enjoyed better fortune:

> For the evacuation flights on May 8 my Bf 109 was still serviceable. I was due to fly it but, as my comrade Reinert was taller than me, I had to let him take the controls and cram into the rear fuselage along with Oberwerkmeister, Ofw. Walter. We were of small enough stature to do this. Reinert then took off, but, over the Gulf of Tunis, spotted a group of Martlets that had just taken off from an aircraft carrier. It was a target he could not resist and despite the extra weight dove on them. He shot down one of these machines and then hastily resumed his journey to Sicily. We were able to land and were pretty relieved when our adventure ended happily enough.

JG 53, for its part, being largely grouped together on its aerodromes, had time to prepare for its withdrawal and would leave last of all, fighting almost to the end. On May 9, Oblt. Jürgen Harder claimed a B-17 near Cape Galle. On that day, 26 German bombers set off to attack the port of Bône.

On May 11, I./LG 1 flew into the Sardinian airfield of Decimomannu to put up 22 aircraft to raid the port of Djidjelli. However, nightfighters were active and a Ju 88 was shot down. On May 12, 30 bombers from LG 1, KG 76, and KG 77 bombed Algiers harbor. A LG 1 Ju 88 failed to return to Decimomannu, victim of a nightfighter. Also on May 12, 1943, General Jürgen von Arnim was captured near Ste Marie du Zit, resulting in the de facto surrender of German troops. On May 13, Italian General Giovanni Messe surrendered with the rest of the Panzerarmee Afrika. The African continent was definitively lost to the Axis.

... while this Me 323 is completely destroyed.

After the fall of Tunis, senior German officers (as here from the Luftwaffe) were evacuated to special camps to be interrogated by Allied intelligence services.

Epilogue

During prisoner interrogations British intelligence uncovered some facts not revealed by Ultra. Thus they learned that a large number of glider student pilots had been grouped together at the end of 1942 in small units sent to Tunisia to reinforce the very depleted Barenthin parachute regiment, serving there as infantrymen. To the surprised British, this was a "real waste of time," as the pilots had received flying training that they were unable to make use of. This was just one indication that the Luftwaffe had deployed every last resource in an African campaign that for the Germans should never developed as it had. When he arrived in Tripoli in February 1941, Rommel had only a handful of aircraft at his disposal, just sufficient to defend Tripolitania. If his opponent was weak, he might even have hoped to win back Cyrenaica. But Rommel chose to focus on Egypt and partially convinced the OKW of the validity of this decision. This transformed a localized conflict into a fresh front of importance for the Wehrmacht, incapable as it was of supporting such an effort. Gradually, X. Fliegerkorps based in Sicily had to give up its aircraft to support Rommel, resulting in the haphazard deployment of units eastward (JG 27) or westward (KG 30, NJG 2). Despite some reluctance, the Mediterranean front attracted JG 27, JG 53, and JG 77, fighter Geschwader which would have assuredly been more useful in Russia. This is not to forget the numerous Luftwaffe bomber units deployed in African skies including the excellent Lehrgeschwader 1.

When the United States entered the war in late 1941 supplying significant amounts of matériel to its British ally, it became impossible for the Afrika Korps to turn the tide. Defeat was therefore inevitable.

Yet, despite the deprivations, suffering, and unrewarded efforts, those on both sides who were fortunate enough to survive and return more or less unscathed from the fighting kept alive memories of the desert campaign. It had been an opportunity for many to discover the beauty of the desert and the charm of its exotic atmosphere. After the war many veterans' associations sprang up, allowing former combatants, and enemies, to come together to remember their battles but also to remember their many comrades left behind in the sands of Egypt, Libya, and Tunisia.

In mid-1943, US Senator Chindler visited the Tunisian battlefields. Here he is seen at the German cemetery at El Aouina where many Luftwaffe airmen were buried.

A French family living in Tunisia poses in 1945 with an abandoned Fw 190, probably in El Aouina. The aircraft has been stripped of all useful parts and is now waiting for the scrap-metal workers to remove the last vestiges of the Luftwaffe in Tunisia.

Sources

Cony, Christophe & Jean-Louis Roba. *Luftwaffe in Colour: The Victory Years 1939–1942*. Casemate Publishers 2016.

Cony, Christophe & Jean-Louis Roba. *Luftwaffe in Colour: From Glory to Defeat 1942–1945*. Casemate Publishers 2017.

Cull, Brian. *Hurricanes over Tobruk*. Grub Street 1999.

Gundelach, Karl. *Die deutsche Luftwaffe im Mittelmeer 1940–1945*. Peter Lang 1981.

Hermann, Hajo. *Bewegtes Leben*. Motorbuch Verlag 1986.

Morzik, Fritz. *Die deutschen Transportflieger im Zweiten Weltkrieg*. Bernhard & Graefe Verlag 1966.

Obermaier, Ernst. *Die Ritterkreuzträger der Luftwaffe. Bd I. Jagdflieger*. Dieter Hoffmann 1989.

______________. *Die Ritterkreuzträger der Luftwaffe. Bd II. Stukaflieger*. Dieter Hoffmann 1993.

Roba, Jean-Louis. *Le Me 323 Gigant*. Lela Presse 2011.

______________. *Werner Schroer, la seconde étoile d'Afrique*, in *Histoire de guerre* N° 33 (2/2003).

Schlaug, Georg. *Die deutschen Lastensegler-Verbände 1937–1945*. Motorbuch Verlag 1985.

Shores, Christopher & Hans Ring. *Fighters Over the Desert: The Air Battles in the Western Desert, June 1940 to December 1942*. Neville Spearman 1969.

Stimpel, Hans-Martin. *Die deutsche Fallschirmtruppe 1942–1945*. Einsätze im Süden. Mittler Verlag 2006.

Units

Aubusson, Charles. "Les yeux de Kesselring: la 2.(F)/123." in *Avions* N° 107 (2/2002).

Gundelach, Karl. *KG 4 General Wever*. Motorbuch Verlag 1978.

Prien, Rodeike & Stemmer *II./JG 27*. Struwe Verlag. S.d.

______________. *Stab & I./JG 27*. Struwe Verlag. S.d.

Hans Ring & Girbig Werner. *Jagdgeschwader 27*. Motorbuch Verlag 1972.

Schlaug, Georg. *II./KGzbV 1 (II./TG 1)*. Kameradeschaft ehemaliger Transportflieger 1989.

Schmidt, Rudi. *KG 26 (Achtung, Torpedo Los)*. Bernard & Graefe Verlag 1991.

Taghon, Peter, *La Lehrgeschwader 1, l'escadre au griffon*. Lela Presse 2017.

Index